D0044365

LOVED AND WANTED

LOVED
AND
WANTED

A Memoir of Choice,
Children, and Womanhood

Christa Parravani

Henry Holt and Company   New York

Henry Holt and Company
Publishers since 1866
120 Broadway
New York, New York 10271
www.henryholt.com

Henry Holt® and 🏛® are registered trademarks of
Macmillan Publishing Group, LLC.

Library of Congress Cataloging-in-Publication Data

Names: Parravani, Christa, author.
Title: Loved and wanted : a memoir of choice, children, and womanhood /
Christa Parravani.
Description: First edition. | New York : Henry Holt and Company, 2020.
Identifiers: LCCN 2020018815 (print) | LCCN 2020018816 (ebook) | ISBN
9781250756848 (hardcover) | ISBN 9781250756855 (ebook)
Subjects: LCSH: Parravani, Christa. | Women college teachers—United
States—Biography. | Mothers—United States—Biography. | Reproductive
rights—United States. | Women—Health and hygiene—United States.
Classification: LCC CT275.P3846 A3 2020 (print) | LCC CT275.P3846 (ebook)
| DDC 306.875092 [B]—dc23
LC record available at https://lccn.loc.gov/2020018815
LC ebook record available at https://lccn.loc.gov/2020018816

Our books may be purchased in bulk for promotional, educational, or
business use. Please contact your local bookseller or the Macmillan Corporate
and Premium Sales Department at (800) 221-7945, extension 5442, or
by e-mail at MacmillanSpecialMarkets@macmillan.com.

First Edition 2020

This is a work of nonfiction. However, names and identifying
details of certain individuals have been changed to protect their privacy.

Designed by Kelly S. Too

Printed in the United States of America

1 3 5 7 9 10 8 6 4 2

For my mother

I must take my stand upon some vantage ground and begin to fight—I must choose between despair & Energy—I choose the latter.

John Keats

LOVED AND WANTED

PART ONE

Everything happens at least
twice anyway, once in the body
and once in the soul.

Irene McKinney, *Past Lives*

Come to New York. My first memory.

Two years old. Too young to know the difference between a hideaway and a hellmouth. Late morning. Mom set breakfast on the table. She went upstairs after, to fold laundry while my twin sister, Cara, and I ate. Mom sat down on her bed, closed her eyes. Just for a moment. Our father's yelling kept Mom up at night. She was always alone with his shouting, never any rest. Cara and I roomed one door down, lucky; we could hold each other to sleep.

You might ask: Your mother slept, a pair of toddlers roaming the house? But haven't you been too tired to stay awake? Haven't you lost sleep over something? My mother did her best with what she was given. She always has. Even now.

Our kitchen had a beautiful oven, an antique with a heavy, white porcelain door. I stood before it atop a footstool, Cara right behind. Four arms on the handle, somehow, we pulled the door down. The metal rack at the bottom slotted through the last rung. The rack was clean, so clean it appeared polished new. The oven's walls were speckled black, like a burned house's frame, but charred with food and smoke. We were twins but I was smaller—I was the one going in. I wore flame-retardant, pink, footed pajamas. Brown smudged my elbows where I'd slid against grease. It was a tight fit. No room to sit up. I pulled myself into child's pose, rump on ankles, holding my weight, hands before me. I was the Christmas ham.

Cara smiled and waved from outside, then the oven's door banged shut. From where I was, this is what I knew: commotion outside the sap-colored, baked-over viewing window. Cara's muffled yell for Mom. A chair rumbling over the floor. Cara's toes at the edge of the chair's seat, which she'd pushed close to the oven's door. She yanked and yanked. The door wouldn't budge. One last try. Cara lost her footing, falling floor-ward. Her elbow turned a knob on the way down. The pilot swished. A cooking-coil glowed orange under me. I pivoted from hand to hand, lifting each when the heat was too much.

I had a choice. The first visceral body-choice I ever made. Which hand to leave to burn against the oven's rack, which to spare. I still have the scar. Let me show you.

Here.

1

It was the last day of my old life. The third week of October 2017. The year I turned forty.

Jo was at school. Iris was at daycare. I didn't know where my husband, Tony, was.

It's peculiar what I can't forget. Our bathroom held the sickeningly sweet smell of geranium-scented cleaner. I wore pants and not a dress. Socks but no shoes. A too-tight blouse. Unwashed hair pinned in a bun above my neck. I sat against a wall, where the taupe paint was scratched, an uncapped EPT developing in my grip. I held the test upside down. I couldn't bear to watch. A gap beneath the door set a rectangle of yellow light across the tub. Two minutes to know what would become of me. Time passed, a whole life. I flipped the EPT over when waiting got harder than knowing. Two red lines on a white strip stared at me. A second test lay in the box. I ripped its foil package open with my teeth. Right between the sink and the commode, I crouched down, swearing in disbelief. I was still breast-feeding twelve-month-old Iris, still recovering from pregnancy and birth, still lonely the way a mother is when she can't find the person she used to be.

I knew when it happened. The deaths of our fathers had brought us close. Tony and I had fumbled to find each other in our unlit bedroom. He'd reached for me and I held him. There are people in life you feel you've known before. I'd never met Tony. He's a big man, a strong man. He weighs one hundred pounds more than me. His eyes are blue, so clear and blue they seem empty and foreign and unreadable. He's a combat veteran, marked emotionally with scars of bullets he survived. Tony prefers life be raw and unpredictable and intoxicating with risk—or so the years of our marriage tell. Tony's father was dead. He didn't know how to say how much loss hurt.

We fucked sweetly in our bed. He didn't pull out. I didn't ask him to. When he comes he unravels. The wall between us drops for a few miraculous seconds. I'd wanted to please Tony. I'd demonstrate my love by taking all of him.

I'd been careless and stupid.

Two more red lines.

I threw the test across the room. Of course, it hit the tile over the bathtub, flying back at me. Our situation was disconcerting. We couldn't afford another baby. We were like most Americans. No savings, no emergency fund, lots of debt. Lots and lots. Professors at West Virginia University, Tony and I held the exact same position. Identical jobs. Tony made more than I did. And he didn't even want the job. He was always trying to quit, looking for shinier work. Hollywood writing work. Like so many women, my money was earmarked to look after the children. Seventy percent of what I took home would go to childcare, if we could find it, which I didn't think we could if we had another baby. It had taken a year and a half for a spot to open in a good daycare for Iris, not an uncommon thing in small towns. Demand exceeds supply. There were so few options. I'd placed Iris on several waiting lists six weeks into my first trimester. Each one was the same: write your name on a line and pray.

Most household tasks and chores fell on me. Night feedings. Bills. Boring paperwork. Someone always needed to be fed or rocked or talked off the ledge of a tantrum. I didn't have time to be pregnant. I divvied minutes. The night before I took the EPT, Tony stood in the living room and lifted our upright Dyson by its handle, looking it over as if it were some rare thing. He tried to unlock the detachable hose, squeezing it. Seven years we'd owned that vacuum cleaner. And then Tony asked me how to turn it on.

Our marriage—like all marriages, I assume—is complex, its own country. In our country, we were fighting most days. We were broke. We were overextended. We rarely touched. Talk was tense even about the good things, anger clipping our voices. We argued so much we forgot the original argument. Our marriage was hung on fantasy. A storybook about freelance writing windfalls. A few things: I won't tell you every detail of my marriage, who was good or bad or hurt the other. For my children. For their relationship with their father. My marriage is part of the story; it isn't the point of the story. Had my husband been a financially stable and faithful, kind hero, the cost of daycare would have been the same, the potential loss of my career the same, the distance and barriers to reasonable health care the same. I can blame Tony for not providing economic stability—or time—for me. The money and time that would have made it plainly possible to safely provide for another child. Reprehending Tony might be briefly satisfying, but to do so is to lose focus, to take an occasion when I was handed shame and doubt solely because I was a pregnant woman, and make it about my husband.

In my tiny windowless bathroom, positive pregnancy test in hand, I thought, this is why women opt out of work. This is why we discourage girls from trying in the first place. I had sex for the first time when I was thirteen, not old enough for sex. I wanted to be a clinical psychologist. The women in my family were waitresses and administrative assistants. I've worried all the years after my first pregnancy scare, how a baby might hold me back.

I'd worked so hard. College, though my family couldn't

afford it (I took on enormous student loan debt). Years and years in graduate school. Now a tenure-track job. Tony was going to quit—we could both feel it coming. I was the stable earner in our household. A third baby at forty and my professional life was over. Moments like these, I want my mom. I tell her most things first. Telling Mom is like telling myself. I phoned her, crying. I didn't want another baby. I wanted an abortion.

"Oh, Christa." Mom sounded disappointed in me, the way I was disappointed. I'd failed her. Mom gave up every dream of her own for me. She'd worked two jobs or more my whole childhood, never any help. At twenty-three, Mom had her tubes tied, right on the cesarean surgical table. That never sounded extreme. After years of my father hitting her, two was enough. Two was the punch line. My father had wanted my mother to abort me. I never thought that fact anything other than a fact. It had nothing to do with me. It never hurt. I'd imagine a curtain drawn. Everything black and blank and peaceful without him.

A long pause.

Mom said if I wanted another baby, I could do it. If I wanted to focus on the children I already had, I could do that. Maybe Mom was right, though I was leery. I'd called her crying and panicked the morning Trump won too. It had been tense between us; Mom insisted the country would be fine, don't be dramatic. Nothing would change. It's always been a man's place. Four years later we still remind each other how correct I'd been. But never mind. Mom reassured me we live in a free country. Choice is a given.

"You're right, Mom." As the adult child of an abused woman, there is a code Mom earned: Don't upset her. Do less harm than good. Take care. Let her know you're safe. "I'll be okay," I half whispered. Where in Mom's house was she? At the kitchen table, a cigarette smoldering in the ashtray, readying for the night shift? "I'll talk to you later. After work." I pressed the red End Call button at the bottom of my phone. For the first time in my adult life, I longed to live at home again. To have the care of Mom's meals, and the electric bill paid.

I went back for the EPT, to the bathroom. The little plastic wand was overturned beside the tub. It looked so small there, and harmless, like a scrap of littered paper. I picked up the test, flipped it over in my palm. Still positive. Lines brighter than before. I balanced on a tightrope strung between defiance and disbelief. I held my phone above the double-red-striped viewing window, snapped a photo, and texted the image to Tony without comment. I didn't want him to *see* the picture. I wanted him to *feel* it. A big fat positive like a kick to the gut.

Surely this news would propel Tony to change. A scare like this would dare him into responsibility. He'd own his part. Make it better. Somehow. I felt powerful as I waited for him to respond to my buckshot, as if my being right could protect us from being broke. But then again, this must be a mistake. I'd laugh about it tomorrow. How I'd frightened myself.

Tony wrote back immediately. "You're joking?" and then, "Baby? Stop." Baby, one pet name he calls me.

"Where are you?" I asked.

"Upstairs."

"You're in the house?"

"Yes, in the office." I used to have an office; Iris's bedroom now.

Tony home all that time, I hadn't been by myself. I gathered no comfort from the knowledge, only questions. Was our house soundproof? Or had Tony heard and ignored me, as a neighbor ignores the inconveniently loud fight next door? To be heard and not helped, the lowest rung of solitude. But then again I wasn't alone, with or without Tony: a tiny rider burrowed in me.

Floorboards two stories up creaked with the weight of my husband. Tony was coming down. Stair by stair. I met him at the banister, a step above the landing. I placed my hand over his hand, on curved walnut wood. "I'm sorry," I said, apologizing for nothing, a girlhood habit. I said it as if getting knocked up was solely my doing. "Hold me," I said. "Please." I looped my fingers through Tony's fingers, pulled him to my level. We stood face-to-face then for a short time. I averted my gaze. Tony's eyes were full of concern. No matter to me. I couldn't see him, as I felt he'd spent years not seeing me.

I didn't want to fight. Not now. I pressed my cheek against Tony's chest. I draped his arms around my shoulders, asked for affection. Tony wore a black cotton T-shirt decaled with a blue dinosaur. I closed my eyes and breathed him in. Seven years of marriage, his body of musk, and soap, and sweat, and sex. A hit of the good stuff.

Tony walked me to the living room and sat us on the sofa. He made his body a perch. I leaned back and into him. Tony's belly was warm, warm and soft. He hooked one leg around mine; we were wrapped. One body. I wasn't going anywhere. Neither of us knew what to say.

Birds squawked outside the front window. Car doors slammed closed on the street. I didn't want Tony to say anything. I needed him to listen. Just silence. But all of a sudden I wanted to pummel Tony, anger out of nowhere, though he did what I wanted by keeping quiet. I thought I might like to slap him. A little zap to the cheek, harmless, so he might feel what I felt. Shocked from his body. But I didn't of course. I lay there with him, arms crossed, fear tickling through me like ants march.

I don't know how much time passed. Enough for the boil to cool. "I'm afraid," I said into the bare-silent room. "I can't do this," though I was unsure what *this* was.

"Baby," Tony said gently, and then buried his face in my hair. "It's your body." My handsome husband. He said nothing else. It wasn't his place. His openness, his mercy pained me. How dare Tony be so good to me now, when it was too late to forget how hair-raising the years before had been.

I loved him. No matter what, we'd lose.

I called my OBGYN and scheduled an appointment. Their office is on the other side of town, and named after a place called Cheat Lake. Summers I'd take Jo and Iris to swim in the Cheat River, just a left off the highway and up Fair Chance Road. We'd walk through shady, mosquito-infested woods, towels tucked under our arms. Bites were worth the dip. The water was always brown and cold. Speed boats churned the river's bottom, swirled it around, like chocolate at the bottom of a glass of milk. Little bits of bark floated at the surface. Jo stood in the waist-high water. Iris sat at the shore shoveling dirt into her mouth. I could pull them back if I needed to.

Why am I telling you this?

In 1994, in the first of two incidents, a deluge of poison water from an illegally sealed underground mine at T&T Coal exploded from a Preston County hillside. The torrent shot into Muddy Creek and merged into the Cheat. Heavy metals lowered the water's pH. The river ran rust orange for miles and miles. Fish and plant life were obliterated. A year later, another blowout. Then the Cheat was one of the most endangered and polluted waterways in the nation.

It took more than twenty years, but now it's swimmable. What was dead is reborn. There are tributaries of fish, native bass and perch. The forest around is lush. The history of reviving the Cheat is long. The short answer is people who loved the land and water rallied. They call themselves the Friends of the Cheat. They didn't turn a blind eye. They raised funds. They fought bad laws. They didn't give up.

2

A nurse called my name at Cheat Lake Physicians. We walked down a pictureless white hall. No chit-chat, though I usually would make some. She opened the door into a windowless, cubicle-size exam room, the middle one in a row of offices built side by side. Its thin walls carried sound. Brochures for pharmaceuticals and illustrations of the body tacked against plaster. I was told to undress, to slip on a paper drape.

"I'm pregnant," I blurted, "or I think I am." Before the nurse would congratulate me, I told her I didn't want to be. "What are my next steps?" The nurse didn't answer. She left the room.

"Lie back," the West Virginia doctor instructed. I would feel something cold, a little pressure. A transvaginal wand would show us. Transvaginal ultrasound is more sensitive than abdominal ultrasound. It requires the vaginal insertion of a probe fitted with a camera, a device many women find humiliating. Early ultrasound is medically unnecessary in routine pregnancy care. But I didn't know that as I lay on the examination table. And I wasn't thinking about other women at that moment, only that I had two little daughters at home to take care of and not enough money or time.

The doctor prepped me. He opened my legs and pushed the wand inside. The ultrasound's monitor crackled, a black-and-white screen resembling poor television reception.

"There it is. See?" The doctor put his finger beside a blinking white speck on the display, a flashing star. "The heart."

My period was two weeks late. I was six weeks gone in all. Had I not been paying attention to my cycle, I might not have known to take a test. "A heartbeat already?"

To call that blinking speck a heartbeat is a misnomer, it turns out; or, as I have come to see it, an outright lie. Implantation occurs about twenty-one days after the start of a woman's last period. At six weeks, there is an undifferentiated embryo the size of a small pebble, and a detectable rhythmic pulsing from that cluster of cells transforms into a kind of pacemaker, which *mimics* a heartbeat. Over the next four to six weeks, what we come to think of as a heart, though even that is not yet a heart, is semiformed. The muscle continues to develop and grow. I didn't know all of that then.

Nor did I know that Utah, Ohio, Missouri, Kentucky, Arkansas, South Carolina, Georgia, Louisiana, Mississippi, North Dakota, and Iowa would all pass "heartbeat bills." If enacted, abortion will be banned with the detection of a "heartbeat," the faux kind, even in the extreme conditions of rape, incest, pregnancy endangering a mother's life, and fetal abnormality. Alabama governor Kay Ivey signed one of the nation's strictest abortion laws. The law criminal- izes abortion after a detectable "heartbeat"; doctors who carry out such a procedure could be jailed for up to ninety- nine years.

That day of the pregnancy test with the West Virginia doctor, I was naive. I still believed what I wanted mat- tered. "I want an abortion," I told him, flat, matter-of-fact, heartbeat-like star notwithstanding.

I shifted my weight. The paper over the exam table crackled like a candy wrapper.

The doctor looked at the floor. He was sorry, he said, he couldn't help. That's just the way it was. He was younger than me. No gray hair. No wrinkles. In another context I might have been attracted to him. He was tall and had toffee brown hair and a strong chin. Was he observing me with pity? I've not forgotten the look on his face. He tilted his head to the side and half smiled, which I mistook as an apology. Being younger, he must have understood this was wrong. I'd always assumed youth meant knowing better.

My pants and undergarments lay rumpled on a chair in a far corner of the room. The young doctor stood up from his little wheelie stool, wished me well, asked me to dress, and then closed the door. He didn't pity me. He didn't feel I'd been wronged. He couldn't help me because he didn't want to. His choice.

I stared at the doctor's door, bargaining. Someone would return to that sterile room and go a second round with me. Another doctor would sort this through. I remained on the table until a nurse knocked. A new patient needed the space.

I gathered myself and walked from the building and to my car. I got inside and engaged the engine. I reached into my pocket and pulled out my phone. I dialed a good friend in California, a writer. I needed someone outside of West Virginia to know what had just happened, to believe it myself. I reported to my friend what was certain. It was the first brisk autumn day. I was forty years old. I had a kindergartener and a one-year-old at home. I was an accidentally pregnant, progressive woman in the reddest state in America.

My friend was quiet for a long time. "Someday you'll leave," she said. "No matter what happens, this will be a story you tell."

"No," I said. "I won't." I wanted to take my words back, pull them from air, crush them in my fist. I felt mortification like a pickaxe to the chest. I was a good mother. A mother who struggled in private. There were rules to obey. A decorum. Allegiance to children first.

3

I drove from the doctor's office, hands trembling, out of body. I was a slip of a person risen to the edge. My skin was all that held me inside. I forgot to turn left over the Pleasant Street bridge for home. I looped town. I passed High Street's old theater, its marquee bare, plywood nailed over the windows and doors. Newcomers always have a plan. Remake the spectacular, historic building into an indie movie house—with a bookstore! Two things we don't have. But the old theater is asbestos-filled, too expensive to clean. The newcomers leave.

I double-parked in front of our house. Jo had hung a skeleton dressed in a straw skirt off a plant hook on the porch. It had glitter-rimmed eye sockets and a sprig of pink hair bowed with a bone. Jo would be Snow White for Halloween. I'd hunted for her perfect dress, the blouse frilled at the collar, plunging sewn across a royal blue sweetheart neckline. She wanted an entourage, Iris as a dwarf, the sidekick. Poor girl. Iris's too-tight outfit was fashioned from scratchy yolk-yellow felt. Orange suspenders hiked the waist.

I lived in a neighborhood called South Park, where a hundred years ago homes were built side by side, all the way up the mountain. Some houses are so close together you can touch your neighbor's window from inside your living room. I could. Our neighbor Kirk always pretended not to see me in rumpled pajamas when I left the curtains open in the morning; I prefer illumination to privacy. He always called, though, if I was upstairs and Kingsley (our Boston terrier) was downstairs on the dining table, eating food scraps I'd been too tired to clear.

I got out of the car and ran up our porch's stone steps. Kirk wasn't home. No car outside. No lamps on. Our town is so small it seemed possible that a person could know a thing about you before you knew it. Kirk was my colleague, a brilliant linguist. He could tell you where any one word comes from. I would think of a phrase and ask him how and when it was born. "Bird on a wire" was the first. Kirk said Leonard Cohen. From that moment on he'd won me. Kirk had three children, something not done among my female colleagues—I would be the only woman in the English department with three children, though several men in the department had three.

Our door's latch was bent and loose. I pushed the door open with my hip. The sun shone inside. Dust from the old oak floor swirled in the light, airborne from the force of my sudden entrance. The house was soundless, a stranger's house. I didn't know what to do with the quiet. I went to the kitchen. I walked the length of it again and again, like an animal on a track. I placed my hands on my belly and talked to the bright star inside me. What I said stays between us, belongs to us. I'll never tell.

I called Maude, an activist doctor, my best friend in Morgantown. Maude is petite, strikingly beautiful, and brown eyed. She raises goats and chickens. She travels out of state to cut and color her long, honey-toned hair. She covers her precision style with a floppy gardening hat. Maude's a mother of four, swears with impunity, and has the loudest laugh in the room. We met for the first time the November before Iris was born. Maude joined our circle of friends that afternoon, mostly women and children, around a bonfire, a new baby strapped to her chest. Jo crisscrossed the smoke-filled yard; her fuzzy leopard-spotted coat smelled of wood for the remainder of autumn. I couldn't stop smiling at Maude, a total stranger. We felt an immediate connection, an easy intimacy. She offered all of herself to me in hopes I would stay and fight.

Maude is from a progressive city due east. A West Virginia outsider, like me. She works in a rural town where the poverty rate is 30.9 percent. She could make twice as much money elsewhere, but she won't leave the people she serves. I needed Maude to tell me I'd heard wrong; my interpretation of what the young doctor said was twisted. But the news didn't shock her. I wasn't mistaken. *You made me love it here*—the unutterable words caught in my throat. I felt betrayed by Maude and by my community of women. They knew there's scant choice for women with unwanted pregnancies in West Virginia—53 percent of pregnancies are unplanned in West Virginia. Nobody in our friend group had talked about it, no matter how many pink hats they'd knitted to protest Inauguration Day. I was last in the family to discover the house had a haunted basement. Maude told me my OBGYN's practice would prescribe an RU486 abortion—I just needed to see the right doctor. I needed to ask by name.

I called the office. "I want to see Dr. X as soon as possible, for an abortion, please." I was raw and scared.

The line went quiet for a moment. "I don't know what you're talking about," the receptionist said dryly. Then more forcefully, "We don't do things like that here."

"But you do," I countered. "You don't know what you're talking about." I castigated the cold voice talking at me. I wondered if she sat at a desk in a cubicle, as my aunts who answered phones all their lives had. Or was she out on the line, one in a row of tabled office workers at the university's medical complex.

"I can get you in two months from now," the receptionist said, amused.

That was too late, as she knew, not least because I told her so right then. A woman must be fewer than eleven weeks along to be prescribed RU486, the abortion pill.

"Please?" I found that I was, absurdly, crouching on the floor in our family room, on my hands and knees. "You seem like a nice person," I lied. This phone call had literally brought me down, without my having given the lowering a conscious thought. What did she look like, the woman with my life in her hands? I imagined short buttery curls, like my grandmother's. Groveling got me nowhere. The receptionist offered me another appointment with the handsome young resident, but not with Dr. X.

An "abortion pill" is a combination drug therapy. Five pills. A dose of mifepristone—a hormone that prepares the uterine lining to shed, and four dissolvable tablets of misoprostol. Misoprostol is taken two days after mifepristone. It softens the cervix and causes uterine contractions. Cramping and bleeding begin between one and four hours later. Heavy bleeding lasts four or five hours. Common side effects of misoprostol are diarrhea, nausea, vomiting, headache, dizziness, back pain, and tiredness. Low fever is normal. Symptoms lighten after three days. Spotting and illness can continue for four to six weeks. Two weeks after taking mifepristone, a doctor examines the uterus to assure the pregnancy has cleared.

Birthright of Morgantown operates in a rickety building upstairs from Gibbie's Pub on High Street, a few blocks from campus. Compass Women's Center is in a plaza adjacent to the mighty Mon River, on Don Knotts Boulevard. Both offices pose the premise of options. Pregnant women are lured in with free over-the-counter pregnancy tests, and an ultrasound if the test is positive. Every state has them, "crisis pregnancy centers"; yours is not immune. They aim to keep pregnant women pregnant, and open as close to a Planned Parenthood as possible. At last formal count, there were 788 real abortion clinics in the United States (fewer now), over a third in California and New York, and 3,500 crisis centers.

The only abortion provider in West Virginia offering out-in-the-open RU486 prescriptions and surgical abortion is in Charleston, a three-hour drive from Morgantown in good weather. I've never gotten anywhere in West Virginia in the time a GPS says. Pitted, mountain-riding roads slow everyone down. For a Charleston abortion, I would drive the distance, see the physician, and wait twenty-four hours to be administered the pill or undergo surgery; six hours of travel, plus hours in-clinic. Then another day to do it again. Twelve hours in the car (conservatively). Four hours in the clinic. Two weeks to clear the pregnancy. A return to Charleston for follow-up. In total: Eighteen hours of driving. Six hours of medical care. Twenty-four real hours for an abortion. Two weeks (conservatively) to recover from RU486.

If Tony traveled with me for the support I needed, who would stay with Jo and Iris? It's suggested, and sometimes required, to bring a companion to the clinic. We had no family in the Rust Belt. Our evening babysitter was a college freshman, and religious. She belonged to Young Life, an organization that promotes celibacy as birth control. The sitter had early-morning classes and homework to prepare. The task of caring for two girls for that long was too much to ask; too much of her time and belief. I couldn't admit what I wanted to do, risking her discomfort. Asking friends to watch the girls so I could go to Charleston to have an abortion felt shameful. (And later on, after everyone knew what I wanted, none of them offered to help.) Would Tony and I stay in a sterile motel as we went through the hardest moment of our marriage, with the girls? What would I tell my boss? Would an abortion qualify me for unpaid medical leave? We don't talk about abortion at work, though we should. I'd missed five days of classroom teaching to attend funerals and vigils. I couldn't ask for more time off. I'd be reprimanded and risk my job.

I have a car. A career. A college education. I am white. I have every advantage. West Virginian women live in poverty at nearly twice the national average, 22.2 percent. Medicaid-funded abortion is illegal. A woman making $17,000 a year will pay $450 to $900 for an abortion, not including transportation, childcare, and lodging. Four weeks of her salary for reproductive care.

Morgantown and Charleston are connected by bus. Each way costs fifteen dollars and fifty cents. The trip is four hours and forty minutes. The total price for travel is ninety-three dollars, twenty-nine hours by bus, and the weight of the journey. There are billboards all around the state, erected by the Women's Health Center of West Virginia. Six women in portrait stare out at passersby, head-and-shoulder renderings in pastel watercolor. ABORTION IN WEST VIRGINIA IS STILL LEGAL, the sign reads. It should read: ABORTION IS STILL LEGAL FOR THOSE WHO LIVE CLOSE. ABORTION IS STILL LEGAL FOR THOSE WHO CAN PAY.

And there I was, pregnant by surprise in Morgantown. A woman who looked from the outside to have it all. I would need to provide for a third child with the negative seventy-five dollars in my checking account at the end of every month. Rent was well over half my take-home pay. Groceries, heat and water, student loans, credit card bills, car payment, and daycare claimed more than the rest. Tony paid our phone bill. I had to ask him for money for basics, which he often didn't provide. Tony hid his finances from me; no matter that I begged. I had no access to his accounts, no knowledge of the funds he had. It was a choreographed fight. We'd agree that his behavior was unfair. Tony would promise to change. I'd wait for the reversal that would never come, back off, and the mood in our house lightened. We'd hold hope in that pause; it felt safe to invest in one another, to reveal ourselves. "I struggle with transparency," Tony admitted again and again. He didn't understand why. And I'd feel sorry for him with every round, because I am soft and kind and open, and because I trust. My finest qualities. I refuse to quit them. Giving up goodness is soul surrender.

The day the receptionist refused to connect me to Dr. X, I curled into a ball on the sofa. *Get up*, I said to myself after not very long. *Stop the pity*. Within the hour, I was online, searching a database of doctors who openly perform abortions in Pittsburgh, the nearest city. I spent all morning calling. No doctor would see me, understandably; I wasn't an established patient. Taking a cold-call abortion patient risks safety. Planned Parenthood in Pittsburgh was two hours away from our house. It upholds a twenty-four-hour waiting period. Pittsburgh wouldn't solve my problems.

Besides, I didn't want to go to Planned Parenthood. I was afraid. In college, twenty years old, my birth control had failed. The pill. I'd used it perfectly. It was junior year. My boyfriend, whom I'd dated since I was fourteen and he was nineteen, lived across the street from Albany's Washington Park, near Planned Parenthood. One day while he was at work I made an appointment. I went. Near the clinic's entry, a man held an enlarged photo on glossy paper. He stepped in front of me. He was tall, and lowered his image to my eye level. His picture showed dismembered fleshy arms and legs. That would be my baby.

"Stop!" I yelled, though his job was done. I turned around and went back to the boyfriend's. I couldn't bring myself to return, though I wanted to. What the man did at the door reminded me of what my father had done to my mother. He'd kicked and punched me with his picture.

Weeks passed. Cara helped me come to the decision to

terminate with a family physician. She assured me of my safety and privacy. I could set myself up for a life where I lived up to my potential.

It was April 1, Fools' Day. I'd asked for sedation, to go under for my abortion, so I wouldn't remember. I was visibly upset in the pre-op room, bawling for what might have been. The version of my life where I had a baby with a partner able to father without heroin's gauzy high. One of the last things I recall is a nurse pushing an IV into my hand. "Try not to cry," she said. "It'll look like you've changed your mind." So I shut it. Fretting over. Tears gone.

A little while later, the doctor fitted my mouth with a mask. "Count backward from twenty," he said. "That's how old you are, isn't it?" I was out before I got to ten.

I waited with other women in the recovery room after, a line of us in beds, all covered with warming blankets. We'd been asked to fill out long forms. To reveal our race, our income, our contraceptives. I refused to fill mine out, my protest. The forms struck me as a kind of control. We deserved privacy. We deserved to grieve without paperwork. Women beside me quietly scribbled their names.

I didn't just walk out of my abortion in my twenties and back into normal life. I bled for weeks. There was cramping and exhaustion. I slept the whole car ride home. When I got home I crawled into bed and cried. I didn't stop crying for days, and not because I'd made the wrong choice, but because sometimes the right choice hurts. There was little to no support for those complex feelings.

I've been waiting to say this for more than twenty years: When we talk about choice, we've been forced to abandon nuance. There are stories of women who need to have an abortion because their baby is incompatible with life, or because their lives are at risk. We hear those women, and we should. That quandary is neat, obvious. No woman should die to give birth. But what about the healthy pregnancies, the unwanted ones?

I'll tell you what I believe. Nobody goes to a clinic or a doctor and joyfully ends a pregnancy. Nobody *wants* an abortion. They do it because they're broke, or alone, or need to care for the children they already have, or because they can't raise a baby; there's no room, no support, no will—they'll be bound to the wrong partner, or place, or job. There's no cruel, callous, or godless disregard for innocence or the sanctity of life. There's no forgetting what ending a pregnancy is, what it means. Abortion doesn't stop when it's banned. American women resorted to unsafe abortions in the millions before it was legal. Some died. Countless suffered. Coat hangers and Lysol abortions are not horror fiction. They're realities.

Isn't that necessity? Isn't that life or death?

What if I'd carried to term, had a child as a college student? They'd have a September birthday, born under a Virgo sun. They'd have graduated college by now. They'd have a father in and out of jail. That boyfriend never stopped berating me for the choice I made—he has a miraculous way of finding me online, even where I block him. There's no cake in autumn, no college, no shared custody. I get to close the message window when my old boyfriend writes.

I should be allowed those facts, those complexities. It has always felt forbidden to think of the child I might have raised, to mourn them as I have. All of this time I've been silent. I worried if I said a thing about my after-feelings, I'd prove the clinic protesters right. I'd prove I was ruined by what I'd done merely by saying I hadn't forgotten it and it was hard. But my suffering wasn't due to my abortion; I was young and scared. I knew I held the weight of choice, shutting myself up to protect it.

But I remember less about my abortion at twenty than I remember about the protester. I'll never stop expecting there to be a man waiting to hurt me. I didn't want to put myself through that again, the fear, the being shouted down. It would've been *possible* to get an abortion in Pittsburgh at Planned Parenthood, but it would have been difficult. Every path seemed strung with a trip wire.

Guess how many times I've been told abortion wasn't out of reach for me while I was living in Morgantown. Multiply the number by ten. It's a part of my story people question. They judge. It used to be hard to explain and defend. I'm learning to be gentle with myself. A surgical abortion at Planned Parenthood in Pittsburgh would have taken the fewest days. How many? Too many. I haven't made the exact count. I don't want to. I shouldn't have to. Calculating feels like apologizing for weakness and stupidity. The very reasons I wanted that abortion—exhaustion, lack of funds, dimming sense of self-determination and confidence—were the things that made it nearly impossible for me to get one.

I should have seen how *easy* this all could have been, but I didn't, because it wasn't.

When Iris was two-and-a-half years old, she stood toes in the Pacific, and a wave took her under, rolled her. I pulled her up and she cried. "It disappeared me, Mommy. It disappeared me." Iris still says with certainty. She won't go back into the ocean, no matter how many times I tell her. I could see her just fine in the water.

I'd been disappeared.

4

Tony arrived home a few hours after I made my last pleading Pittsburgh doctor call. It was late afternoon, well after I'd returned from the visit with the young Cheat Lake physician. Tony found me sitting at the dining room table, head in hand. He stood behind me and encircled his arms around my shoulders. He rested his chin on top of my head. I told him what I'd learned of my options. He didn't believe me. I wouldn't have believed either, the day before. But there we were.

He was hopeful about another baby. We'd be an animated, loving, rough-and-tumble bunch. A five-pack. "But the money," I said. "I can't bring another child into a house with such tenuous finances." There we were, falling and falling in a fearless fight again, like superheroes wrestling through the sky in a comic book.

A few hours later the phone rang. It was Dr. X. Maude had called them on my behalf. Tony and I sat at opposite ends of the table. I set my phone on speaker. Tony listened in. I needed a witness, not for proof, but to understand. The doctor said they could end my pregnancy by prescribing RU486. I shouldn't tell a single nurse—or anyone on staff—why I sought care. Not too long before, they'd helped a teenager have a surgical abortion. A nurse had seen it on the girl's chart. The discovery caused upheaval; staff and nurses filed a formal complaint against the doctor. Dr. X feared for their job and probably for their life. This, though abortion is legal. If I had complications, I'd be better off calling Dr. X on their cell phone. Abortion has turned into a whisper-network procedure all over the country, a thing for people in the know. Dr. X provides abortion quietly and bravely, as many other physicians in the United States do, just not out in the open.

The doctor was required to provide mandatory counseling advising me against the procedure. They were willing to do so over the phone. Dr. X went into their office. They said they needed to close their door. They recited in a hushed voice a list of all the bad things that could happen to my body should I terminate, the least of which was regret.

It all made me uneasy. A medical procedure shouldn't be a hidden thing. There are always risks. I worried the nosy nurse would see my name. Would I be outed and derided in such a small town? I worried I might suffer infection.

I worried for the emotional aftermath too, for the sadness and the indignity. These barriers to abortion left me feeling I'd done wrong. I had the sense of myself as a person who wished to commit unspeakable acts, who deserved every hard thing to come my way. I don't know if the feeling passes. I'm still in the room with that ghost.

The night I talked to Dr. X, I scanned the internet for herbal and prescription home methods: pennyroyal, savin, tansy, rue. I sleuthed websites claiming to mail mifepristone. They asked for money wires to China and India. I imagined ingesting mystery pills before bed, then never getting up again. The decision of whether to keep or terminate a pregnancy brings us to the brink of life and death, and to our limits and desires. I couldn't travel to Charleston. I couldn't order medication and doctor myself. I couldn't accept Dr. X's help. What if something happened to me? I have children who need their mother. I needed the safety of my own bed, and to watch over my daughters asleep in their dim rooms. I needed an abortion to preserve what we had.

A year later, I talked to a local activist, told her about Dr. X. I waited for her to tell me that I'd been dramatic, ridiculous; the imagined qualities I lambasted myself with. But she didn't. Women suffering botched home abortions have been turned from Morgantown emergency rooms, she said. Second thoughts were wise.

Most women seeking abortion care are already mothers. The 2015 Turnaway Study, housed at the University
of California San Francisco, followed the impact of cur-
tailed reproductive choice on children: existing children,
children born from an unwanted pregnancy, and future
children. Turnaway compared one thousand women who
received abortion care with an equal number of women
who were denied a wanted abortion. Children with mothers denied abortion were significantly more likely to be
homeless, go hungry, and fail to meet developmental mile-
stones. They lived below the federal poverty level, at four
times the average. They more often dropped out of high
school, suffered mental health problems, and engaged in
criminal or delinquent behavior as teens and adults.

Mothers in the Turnaway Study felt seized and clois-
tered, and pined for the "old days." They had harder times
bonding with their babies.

They worried about means of support. For good reason.
Turnaway found "being denied a wanted abortion results in
a reduction in full-time employment that lasts about four
years; an increase in public assistance that persists until
women are timed out of these programs . . . an increased
likelihood that women don't have enough money to pay
for food, housing, and transportation; and, finally, an
increased chance that women are raising children alone."

Women denied reproductive health care more often
experience serious complications: eclampsia, depression
and anxiety, hip and joint trouble, PTSD, suicidal ideation,

and even death. They remain leashed to abusive partners. They are twice as likely to suffer domestic violence. The Brookings Institution found women carrying unintended pregnancies experience the highest rates of domestic violence, during and after pregnancy. Judgment has nothing to do with it. Anyone can fall prey to coercive partnership. Abortion makes it easier for women to escape. Custody laws, increased financial dependence, the awareness that children need their fathers, even fathers hurting mothers. Leaving can feel hopeless.

O Let me tell you of foolish love

Tony and I traveled in the same circle before we met, New York creative types. He was a writer of stature. I was a graduate student. Tony was known in a way I have never been known. We met in late September 2010. Tony was immediately good to me. I couldn't believe my luck. Tony wanted me. A family with me. He treated me to elaborate dinners out in a whiplash speed courtship.

A month after we met, Tony slipped a full-carat solitaire diamond ring over my finger. "Yes," I said. "Yes." I had no father. Cara died when we were twenty-eight, five years before. I was desperate for family. My handsome husband-to-be offered me what I'd lost.

The day before we married, Tony confided he had no money. It was a confession delivered without hubris, but a bit of a dare.

"Not even a penny?" I'd asked, confused. Tony had had a big success with his first book. He couldn't explain what he'd done with the proceeds. I knew nothing of that world. I took him at his word.

There was the nagging feeling of what he'd concealed. I pushed it aside. I promised Tony I'd carry us on student loans; he'd get back on his feet, it didn't matter if he was broke. What mattered to me was that I loved him, and I did love him, better than I loved myself. I didn't understand. Tony had blown large sums of money, was capable of blowing large sums of money. His credit was fried. But I'd never had any money. Who was I to judge? Love. I bet on love. How does the old song go . . .

5

It was the thirteenth week of my unplanned pregnancy. Second trimester. A week after Thanksgiving. University office hours. I sat at my campus desk, door closed, waiting for students to knock. Hunks of brown dust-like material covered the desk's varnished wood. Fallen through holes in the drop ceiling, like flour from a sifter.

My phone rang. Dr. X's number scrolled over the display. Another loop in the knot pulled tight. I stared at a forty-by-fifty-inch framed photograph I'd taken years ago of Cara and me. It hung beside a window on my office's west-facing wall. We're gripping hands in a cornfield in the picture, mud caked onto the hems of the matching white hooded cloaks we wore. It's early blue evening in New England, our foreheads pressed together—in another time

I was a photographer and a sister. I'd run between Cara and the timer mounted on my lens. Take after take, I'd tried to get the picture right. Fifteen years had passed; a stranger lived that life. The space between Cara and me in the picture is person-shaped, but small. I used to think the void meant what was missing.

Four rings and I answered the call. Dr. X had the results of a blood test calculating probability of fetal abnormality. I clenched my jaw. I stiffened my neck and shoulders. How I'd worried for this child. My age. The stress. Pregnancies one after another; the baby was at higher risk. I carried concern like a rock in my chest. "It's okay." Dr. X sensed my worry. "Healthy. You have a healthy baby."

I exhaled. Relief so potent I felt lifted. We were lucky. Spared.

Dr. X asked if I wanted to know the gender? I did want to know, though it would be impossible to leave that moment free. I saw a him. Imagined his face. Attached myself. A son. My son coming. My boy.

The same beat; a son for Tony at the moment he'd lost his father. Our boy was at a door between West Virginia and the spirit world, if there is such a thing, if I chose to believe, which I didn't.

The basement door was wide open when I returned home from work. A box packed with holiday decor sat ransacked in the dining room. Jo and Iris ran around it, jingle bells tied with red ribbon around their necks. Christmas was coming. Tony pulled our giant silver tinsel tree from a spider-infested shelf under the basement stairs. "You okay?" I shouted down into the sour-smelling cavern. Branches poked through cardboard, rubbing Tony's neck red as he shouldered the box. I'd bought our ten-foot tinsel wonder one Black Friday. Morgantown winters are rainy and gray, snow scarce. Silver is a beckoning. It promises otherworldly grace.

I unfurled the tree. Worked hours pulling it apart. It's a bear of a thing. Hoisting it alone is nearly impossible. Back and forth, back and forth—I close-danced the tree, my face smashing its middle. My hands deep in, I grabbed the base. Metal scratched my hands and forearms. Jo leapt and twirled around the room. I swore at Christmas. I was done when Jo stopped dancing to point out the tree's bald spots.

We baked my grandmother's sugar cookies. The recipe is handwritten in black ink on age-browned paper. My grand-mother tucked her instructions inside a small, pictureless cookbook of standard Sicilian dinners. We got three steps in. Jo left to imagine at her dollhouse. Iris clanged metal bowls against the kitchen's stone floor. The puppy, Kings-ley, stayed underfoot, snout to the ground, licking crumbs. My mother's mother cooked by intuition. A thumb of but-ter. Sugar fills the bottom of the bowl. Wrist-deep flour. Her secret ingredient: rum-soaked fruit rolled in.

Jo taped Santa's list to the mantel. Iris pulled all orna-ments within her reach from the garish silver branches. I rearranged the glass globes higher and higher, until two feet of tree was naked, spare white lights.

Albany is nine hours by car from Morgantown. I hadn't told anyone, but I'd called the gynecologist who gave me my college abortion. They could schedule me for a dilation and extraction abortion the Tuesday before Christmas. The cost was three thousand dollars. I didn't have the money. I requested and was granted a credit line increase on a previously maxed-out card. I'd need to find a ride home from the surgery center. I could ask an old friend from high school who still lived in town, I thought. A brutal surprise out of nowhere, but it was what it was.

Dilation and extraction abortion, also known as D&E, is performed between fourteen and twenty-four weeks of pregnancy. The Centers for Disease Control and Prevention estimates 7.6 percent of abortions occur in the second and third trimesters, 2.1 percent of those between sixteen to eighteen weeks. Numbers decline steeply as pregnancy progresses. Osmotic dilators begin a D&E. Rods of brown seaweed thinner than twigs are inserted into the cervix. Body moisture swells the rods, slowly opening the womb; two or three days wide. Sedation, vacuum aspiration, forceps, and a curette—a long-handled, sharp-edged surgical spoon—are needed during the twenty-minute procedure.

UCSF medical sociologist Katrina Kimport studied the reasons women seek second-trimester abortions. Out of twenty study participants, six discovered severe fetal abnormality during early second-trimester tests. The remainder "wanted an early abortion and tried to get one but were unable to do so because of the substantial obstacles placed in their path." Barrier states, like mine.

A D&E would send me home to Albany for Christmas, but without the girls. I couldn't care for two rowdy kids while also recovering from surgery. Mom would think the situation strange, though she'd be delighted that I'd be home for Christmas. After Cara died, Mom stopped celebrating holidays, never even adorning a tree. Mom would have supported me in the hard truth, held me in that moment. But upholding Mom's belief that I was okay, not only okay in my pregnancy, but in my life, seemed necessary. Mom had attached herself to the idea of a grandson. My ever-expanding family was a sliver of proof that living wasn't all about dying. So I had hidden everything: the money, the fighting, the desperation, how little I felt I mattered in the place where I was raising daughters. I'd have to tell Mom I'd miscarried. But I couldn't bloody my childhood bed in secret, Mom one room over, watching reruns of *Law and Order*. I'm a lousy liar.

I'd have to bleed elsewhere.

I could maybe return to Santa Monica, where I'd had Iris during summer break. The cost of the abortion was the same as in New York. A friend had offered her spare room for free. I'd have to figure out how to pay for the flight, which I couldn't fathom affording. I could seek care with my former Los Angeles OBGYN; I called Dr. Y to ask if I could be seen in my condition. I told her of those last weeks of denial and waiting. She held her disbelief through silence for longer than felt comfortable. "Women see me and think they're being persecuted for having to wait a few hours, and they are," she said. "Come home. I'll take care of you."

My California plan went as far as imagining Tony, Jo, and Iris stringing our fake tree with popcorn and cranberries, Dr. Y putting me under on the sunnier coast. After, I'd sit in Santa Monica more alone than I'd ever been, the too-blue ocean mocking me.

Human awareness is guided by sense: sight, smell, taste, hearing, touch. The cerebral cortex forms perception, intelligence, memory, language, and what some call "consciousness." Ten states, including West Virginia, have banned D&E abortion. Lawmakers championing those bans espoused unprovable, false pain science. Countless studies state it's unlikely a fetus perceives pain before the third trimester because the cerebral cortex is yet to be formed.

False fetal pain theories have obscured the real pain suffered by women impeded from first-trimester abortions. And yet early abortion restrictions guarantee more second-trimester abortions, and thus more (imagined) fetal pain. What of the psychological pain of women who must wait for a wanted abortion? The pain of a distraught mother on her living children? The days of dread and confusion? The humiliation of seeking hidden options? The self-blame? The second-guessing?

In *The Argonauts*, Maggie Nelson writes, "Feminists may never make a bumper sticker that says IT's A CHOICE AND A CHILD, but of course that's what it is, and we know it. . . . We're not idiots; we understand the stakes. Sometimes we choose death." And sometimes we cannot. A person the size of an avocado or pear—depending on which app or book you read—sucked his thumb in me, had fingerprints and cupid-bow lips. Pain. The truest pain I've ever known. Pain in exact proportion to the vibrancy of the imagined body inside of mine. That's what I felt. And I couldn't bring myself to schedule a D&E. Could you?

I HID THE pregnancy at work for as long as I could.

My students noticed my pregnancy with my son before my colleagues did. I taught budding writers who wanted not to be rude by mentioning the obvious, eyes traveling down. My pregnancy was crass. Nobody wanted to say it. There's the wives' tale that pregnant women ought not get upset. Exposure to sadness or rage might boil the baby. Even reasonable women I know yield to it. There's nothing of that notion that isn't a muzzling. It's another way to keep women at home, trapped in themselves, hiding their reasonable feelings. Under the guise of what's best for baby, mothers are hard-pressed to admit how dark it gets. But that doesn't stop it from getting dark. It stops us from opening the curtains. I teach nonfiction. We read about terror, violence, death, sex, poverty, and loathing from the inside out, and other things. My students hand me their baby-boiling secrets.

The first week of December during my unplanned pregnancy, Katha Pollitt, a feminist writer, came to give a lecture at our university. I was on the small committee who'd invited her. Our faculty planning board had been tasked with the mission of raising morale after the 2016 presidential election. We'd made a short list of speakers, Pollitt the top choice. A few weeks after Pollitt accepted our offer, we discovered her talk would be on the state of abortion in the country: *Abortion: Truth and Post-Truth*. The committee chair announced this to our room of six planners. I'd never imagined Pollitt's talk, the subject; I was too exhausted to consider much of anything, including experts focused on my current life crisis. Was I the only one who flinched at this unsurprising news? University budget cuts had been profound. Nearly all the money, and especially our salaries, at the state's mercy. The brass wouldn't like Pollitt here. Nobody else seemed concerned.

Tony sat beside me in the last row, Pollitt behind the lectern. When I ask him about that night now, he tells me he had no idea I was uncomfortable. Yet I gripped my chair. I sat expressionless, all but for my eyes, which surely held the look of a fever dream. Partners, maybe more than anyone, see what they want of the beloved. Pregnancy as demonstration of devotion. Belly pushing against my too-tight dress, tights itching my thighs, bra cutting into my back; Tony squeezed my hand. I thought he knew. I thought he was afraid too.

The group listened intently to Pollitt. I stared as if from the end of a tunnel. She read from a stack of papers on the podium. I skipped from thought to thought. *Who gets accidentally pregnant at forty? Do my colleagues know? If they do know, do they politely assume a large family is what I want, then backbite me at the Xerox machine? Maybe the gossip is that I want another semester of paid leave, a baby for a few months off. Do people think I want to get out of West Virginia that much—getting knocked up is a scheme I had? And who let those people in here?* Protesters. They occupied the row adjacent to me. *Isn't there a rule for that? Of course there is a rule for that. Free speech.*

Led inside by a conservative member of our history faculty, the protesters had arrived quietly, but in mischief, as if they'd each swallowed the bird. Flimsy signs with pictures of bloody fetuses and catchy anti-choice slogans propped on their laps: *Your mother was pro-life. Speak for the weak. Where there is life, there is hope. Wait it out, it gets better.* I was too timid to speak during the Q&A. All I had were questions. The depletion that comes with a full-bellied, unintended pregnancy—with every swift kick and turn that is the miracle of your baby thriving—it's a primal reminder the state believes it knows better than you. You know less than nothing, and even less about yourself. I sat quietly in my last-row chair, imagining giving each protester a roundhouse kick.

I'd done what good girls do, by default, and remained slow with child. Caged by my body, reduced to a vessel, I was rage filled, not going easy. I listened to Pollitt and it felt as if someone had slipped a bag over my head from behind. I wanted to kick and punch and scream my way out. I've long admired Susan Sontag's *Regarding the Pain of Others*: "Nobody can think and hit someone at the same time." I recite Sontag's line to Jo and Iris sometimes, hoping to keep them from pulling hair, slapping, and pinching. Consider first. Strike only when necessary. Mind over body. Advice is easier to give than receive. I didn't want to think that Christmas. I wanted to burn the house down, plow the forest over, and flood High Street. But I was no master of violence.

I was thin, yet my body hung heavy on me. I had to pee. I could only breathe by half.

6

In *Pro*, the book that brought her to WVU, Katha Pollitt wrote of prenatal sonograms:

> Sonograms distort reality in another, more subtle way: you can only take a picture of the embryo/fetus if you erase the body of the pregnant woman. As with the famous optical illusion of the duck-rabbit, you can't see them both at the same time: either you see a rabbit or you see a duck. In a sonogram the fetus is the subject, the woman is the background; the case for its personhood is made by turning her into gray-and-white wallpaper.

But that was my wish, exactly. A complete, final eradication of self. The baby could thrive in spite of me. I was nineteen weeks along now. A little dome beneath my dress rounded over my thighs. That's it. I had trouble gaining weight, though I force-fed. Each month the nurse weighed me. She penciled in the number and shook her head. I was well under the recommended size. Some people eat when they're sad, betrayed, or demoralized. I forget how to live; no hunger, thirst, or sleep.

During my pregnancies with Jo and Iris, my middle went round with girls, hard and impossibly, tenderly large. Cats use their whiskers to determine whether they'll fit in a place. I had no barometer or instinct, no way of knowing; I was thrilled to be place-lost, big with daughters. I had once believed a thin body meant power; all angles, and eyes set large over gaunt cheeks. Men loved to grip my hip bones as I lay under them, never my flesh. I thought my hollows made worthy touchstones. Slender bodies were proof of endurance and grit, a disregard of hunger in service of sex. So I ate not enough, to allow myself more power, more agency. In a world for men, that's how I knew how to survive. Thinner, I held the illusion of control. Otherwise known as: anorexia nervosa.

Pregnant with daughters, I'd belly-bumped walls and doorways. Stuffed swollen into my clothes like a sausage; my pleasure and luxury. My new power. A truer power. This third time, I backslid into my eating disorder. I was bones again, back to the old lie about slightness and command. I was counting the weeks to full term, only halfway there. Get out when you can, I thought to this one; this body is no place to live. I wished him born because I wanted to spare him. He was better off out of me.

And not only because I was thin and tired—though I worried about my low weight. And not because I didn't want him with me, inside. But for the fact that he was a son. I never knew with Iris and Jo—eighty-two weeks of pregnancy with daughters, I never fortified the illusion of their safety outside of my womb.

I was afraid before my daughters were born. I had them and haven't stopped worrying.

Girls crumpled in cornfields. Girls never coming home. Girls catcalled. Girls mortified in red-stained pants when their times come. Girls picked last in school; girls raising their hands highest. Girls pretending not to know the answer become women who let men order the entree. Women forgiving too much. Women forgetting themselves.

I relived the denial of my wanted abortion like an amnesiac. My local friends took a step back each time I recounted the tale, which was every time I saw them. I came into the room, dragging my sadness, causing a great amount of discomfort. Their silent prayer that I'd shut up was louder than the dozen or so kids screaming down the hall.

My West Virginia friends all owned homes and had bountiful gardens of kale and tomatoes, and savings plans.

Their husbands mowed the lawn. Some had vacation prop-
erty. I wanted that. The vacation. The something to fall
back on. Our Trump-supporting landlord liked to remind
us of our tenuous place, how disposable tenants are. He
sent an email about late rent once, during the earliest
hours of the first of the month, right after Tony had published an op-ed about gun control in the *New York Times*. I
genuinely worried we'd have three children and nowhere
to live.

"Women should be able to choose," my friends said,
all in agreement, nervously chopping vegetables for the
crudités, or fruit for the children. "But I'd never do such
a thing, never have an abortion." They sipped their wine,
needing to understand my story as merely a demonstration for the right. "You didn't really want to terminate," I
got told.

I wasn't really being asked, but I always answered hon-
estly, anyway, a barbarism when spoken over my ever-
expanding middle. Parties never got comfortable.

Nobody wants to admit defeat. My pregnant belly was
proof. We're on the losing side of women's health care.
My friends turned the other way. Even the women thought
me hysterical. They may call me whatever they wish in private. *Hysteria*, from the Greek word *hystera*, "uterus." Not
untrue in my case.

I was living the punch line of a cosmic joke. Tony wasn't
alone in his father-son death-bind. I'd conceived the night
before I said goodbye to Pete, that man who was as close

to a father as I'll ever have. I flew home to New York to him, seed knitting in me. Pete had late-stage, rapidly moving stomach cancer. His diagnosis came a week after we lost Tony's father. Mom stayed with Pete after he'd agreed to take morphine. They waited for the end in his room together, through hallucinations.

The day Pete and I said goodbye, we sat together in the sun for hours on his farmhouse's back porch. It faced thick woods filled with autumn birds. We gripped hands. Pete's big hand seemed small in mine. I told Pete his love had been the biggest revelation of my life. He'd shown me I was worthy of a father. I told him I'd take him with me to every summit from that day forward, and into the natural world that thrilled him. He belonged with me at every vista, even the ones at home.

Mom and Pete met at the public pool when I was thirteen. It was right after my stepfather walked out and never came back. Mom and I laid a blanket out on the grass, right beside Pete and his son, a boy of three with mussed hair and his mountain-climbing daddy. Pete was Mom's junior by more than a decade. Their romance failed. Their love never did. Through death and joy and children, Pete was there. He watched me graduate from college. He held me as I huddled on the floor at my mother's house, legs pulled to my chest, cold with grief. Cara dead. A heroin overdose. Twenty-eight years old. Gone. And when Tony and I eloped in a blizzard, only three months after having met, snow piled high through Manhattan, transport at a standstill, cabs crashed into shoulder-high snowbanks, Pete saw my mother through white and wind. Mom implored me to reconsider—I was a modern woman. Couldn't I just live in sin? Pete kept his opinions to himself. He stared at Tony and me in our wedding garb, as one might look over a steep cliff with a view.

A week after we married, I was late. I look at our wedding pictures now and I see three of us, Jo hiding. The last afternoon of my life before motherhood, I peed on a stick pregnancy test in a movie theater bathroom. The result was a big blue plus sign. Thirty-two years old, I felt I'd won the time lottery. I sped the rocky fertility speedway, frantic to the finish line. Why did I ever think it was a race? I called Pete from inside the stall. "Tony and I have no money, no history," my voice echoed off the partitions. "But I want a family." I couldn't stop smiling. "Stability."

"The worst thing that happens," Pete answered, "is you eventually lose a guy and you get a baby." More than an even trade.

The lights were down in the theater when I slipped back into the seat beside Tony's. He handed me a bucket of popcorn and a box of candy. I took a bite of each, waiting for *The Fighter* to roll.

Pete and I would have had a good laugh about my getting pregnant again, broke as ever and just as he was dying. "Pregnant," I'd say, holding him tighter than I should. "After losing you? What does that even mean?"

"It means you didn't use birth control." Pete would laugh, put his hands on my shoulders, and push me back. He'd hold me in his great green-eyed gaze. "Make it mean what you want."

7

I gave our son a name. Keats. *A thing of beauty is a joy forever . . . Full of sweet dreams, and health, and quiet breathing.* I let myself love him. I played him music. I talked to him, a constant and sometimes wordless body conversation. "Good sunny morning, boy," I'd say. It didn't matter if the day was rain. It was never the feeling it was me against Keats, my life for his life. We both lived in my body. We both needed that body to be considered and cared for. He heard all about his sisters. I promised Keats he belonged and was wanted in our family. I promised my son I would protect him. I knew how hard that would be. *Knowledge enormous makes a God of me . . . As hot as death's is chill, with fierce convulse / Die into life.*

Late in my second trimester, I switched to a midwife

outside of Dr. X's practice, a respected practitioner in our community. I wanted a new start. I felt captively sad seeing Dr. X after our RU486 history. I hoped the new midwife would find no abortion notes on my chart—I hoped there were no notes. No proof. It was safer for all that my request lived in shadow. With Jo and Iris, I'd looked forward to monthly visits to the midwife. I got to be with family and say hello. Those days shined with potential.

I dreaded prenatal appointments with Keats. Everywhere felt tender, bruised. My anger over having not been able to choose had transformed into fear. As a parent it is nearly essential to have the fantasy of the illusion of control when it comes to your child's well-being. It's a daydream that keeps us from going mad with worry. West Virginia ranks one of the nation's highest for infant and child mortality. The Centers for Disease Control and Prevention lists birth defects, preterm birth, and pregnancy complications as top reasons for infant death. Curtailed-reproductive-freedom states have poor outcomes for infants and children. Michael Hiltzik writes in the *LA Times*, "The correspondence is unmistakable, and not hard to explain: Those states' governments also show the least concern for maternal and infant health in general, as represented by public policies."

"Here we go," I said to Keats as we walked into exam rooms together. "I don't know what happens next." It was a routine. The midwife touched me. I recoiled. She pulled a yellow measuring tape taut against my belly, counted weeks in inches. We listened through sonar. Keats's heart galloped, a lone foal. I cried every time. The midwife didn't ask why.

Also late in this second trimester, Jo got a crimson fighting fish. Moonlight swam to the bowl's edge. Jo stroked the glass. Moonlight as "he" was a concept we worked through. Fighting fish, the lavish ones, all boys. Female fighting fish are brown and small, undecorated. Jo thought only girls could be pretty. I opened my laptop and showed Jo the evidence: pond-floor pictures of Moonlight's stunning brothers in water. She shrugged. Her attention would turn at a dizzying pace. "But is this the fish we eat?" She sprinkled fish flakes over Moonlight's water. "It's not, Mommy? Right?"

"Right."

Jo set Moonlight's bowl beside a window; he needs to see outside. Sun lifted the threaded electric blue of Moonlight's red, water-plumed fin. "I'm never having babies." Jo rolled fish flakes into the silverware drawer. "Too much work." My daughter watching me, observing what I'm afraid to name; the children will think themselves my penalty, my wardens. Jo visions herself as both fish and owner. Daughter and mother.

A YouTube video of a 4-D ultrasound obsessed me around that time. I couldn't stop watching as I grew with Keats. A mother places her hands on her belly. The camera takes an inside view of amber skin and glowing blood. Baby leans to Mom's touch, a picture of convincing grace. An irrefutable, affecting moment. I told Keats good morning. The greeting was for me. Moonlight doesn't understand a girl's love. The baby in the video doesn't understand mothers or sound. Moonlight doesn't know the concept of beyond the house. The baby in the video moves with precognizant potential. Moonlight can't remember the heat reward of Jo's hand. Jo infuses the relationship with significance, which doesn't diminish it, or make her care any less true.

A TWENTY-WEEK SCAN is when you (hopefully) discover your baby has all parts in the right places, they're growing. You get a picture. The three-dimensional image will approximate no one's likeness in your family. You might pretend otherwise. I supplicated my way into a sonography slot. The cusp of nineteen weeks is early. I needed to see my son. Was he shielded from my too-small body?

I sat in a corner chair at WVU's radiology center, ready to know.

I'd taken a place beside a wall of windows facing Walmart. Beyond the glass, a mother pushed a cart with towering paper towels and toilet paper. Cellophaned goods wobbled back and forth. I had the feeling I shouldn't stare, though I was unseeable. The woman craned her neck to each side of packs of Bounty, young daughters ahead, weaving around parked cars. Mother's lips crooked—yelling through the side of her mouth like a ventriloquist.

She was my kind. *Knock it off. Get over here. And yesterday.* She looked to have said.

A thin brown-grassed hill intersected the medical complex and the big-box store. The woman heaved her cart over, roller wheels shaking, then ran behind metal racing down my side of the lot. I've sworn up that hill more times than I care to admit. I never learn to park on the right side. Her girls sprinted ahead. Mom took chase. Another day at Walmart, fearing children will be run over in the parking lot. The sisters waited by a black sedan. Mom fished a fob out of her pocket, hurried over. *Click. Click.* The girls climbed in. Mom buckled them. She relaxed beneath her maroon puffed jacket, a release more of face than body, eyes untensed. Flustered doesn't equal ungrateful. Knowing doesn't ensure believing.

It was late in the day, the end of appointments. A uniformed woman in a burgundy utility apron swept the already-clean floor with a long-handled push broom. We were alone, save the receptionist at check-in vigorously typing at her keyboard. The heat-dry room seemed infested with Lysol. No free air. An automatic door opened each time someone walked down the hall. Fresh cold blew in like a haunt.

It was getting dark. A round, white-faced clock hung on the office's waiting room wall. The second hand ticked loudly, a pulse. I tapped my fingers against the table in time.

A white cargo van pulled up to sonography's curb. An armed officer stepped out of the passenger's side. He walked around the van's back, pulled open double doors. A line of men in pale-blue jumpsuits ducked out, their hands cuffed and feet shackled. They'd traveled from the high-security federal prison in Hazelton, a half hour away. Inmates call United States Penitentiary Hazelton "Misery Mountain." It's a huge stone building built on a flat between obscenely picturesque hills. Razor wire circles the fence around its perimeter. It's one of the most dangerous prisons in the country. Trump slashed funds to prisons nationwide. Hazelton lost one hundred and thirty-seven workers in his cut. The place was overcrowded and understaffed before; workers burned out on long hours and risk.

I was led past Hazelton's inmates and into a sonography room. I got on the table and hiked up my dress. The tech covered my waist in cold jelly, pressed a wand against my womb. There he was, like a photo in negative, black-and-white Keats on the screen. He kicked and turned, flexed and yawned. Hair brightened around his head; Jo and Iris were bald babies. Keats jerked in time with hiccups. His heart drummed. The technician worked quietly. We both marveled at my son. Keats measured a week ahead, grown well in spite of me. He had long legs and a plump belly. The tech tried to capture his image. He crossed one arm over his chest, like a person saying the pledge. His other arm covered his face, a paparazzi block.

"He wants to surprise you," the tech said dryly. "This is the best I can do." She handed me my test shot. My son was an elbow over a flesh blob. "Sorry about that. It's disappointing, I know, I know." It's okay, I told her. I'd just wanted to see him safe.

"Pictures are keepsakes." The tech smiled. "You'll love these!" I was in sudden possession of six images, all of my son's penis. "His most important part." Two girls. I don't have a single ultrasound view of a vagina. "Everyone wants a boy. Boys are easier."

I stared at my son in sonogram. It's inevitable, I thought. I will disappoint. Keats would learn value in reverse, worth as betrayal. He'd spend years enraptured with his mother, as children do, only to discover he'd loved the pauper. I wondered when the moment would strike. Would I be bandaging his knee? Sleeping him slung over my chest? Shouting at him for being naughty? It would come like a bolt, my son realizing he's more important than me. The person he'd trusted to protect and nurture him. Me. I was worth less, his sisters too. I don't sink the moon nor lift the sun. All certainty must fall away with knowing, a brutal heartbreak, like discovering there's no God.

I dressed and left. The Hazelton men shuffled out of the waiting room. The guard lined them against the wall farthest from me. Each were called, one by one, escorted to the van to leave. It was hard not to look. None of the inmates even tried to meet my gaze. I wondered how we'd each arrived there.

Years before, our car rolled through drought-brown Los Angeles. Josephine wanted to know where the road ended, if the road ended at all. Tony thought it over. *The road ends in New York*, he said. *It starts there too.*

PART TWO

Because freedom, I am told, is nothing but
the distance between the hunter and its
prey.

Ocean Vuong,
On Earth We're Briefly Gorgeous

8

We used to live in a Santa Monica bungalow twenty-one blocks from the Pacific Ocean. Josephine was three years old. Iris was an idea. This was two-and-a-half years before I became pregnant with Keats. It was 2015. We'd taken a chance, broken the lease on our irreplaceably inexpensive New York apartment. A job in television looked to be on the horizon for Tony. The work didn't materialize. Hollywood jobs are like that. There and then gone.

We are not the first nor will we be the last to go broke in California. Packed up in latest night, unsold screenplay, or gone belly up on a tech investment, I saw neighbors gone before sunrise, before the usuries. Other neighbors went on in their yoga gear, willfully ignorant, as if the house across the street wasn't empty. A woman my age lived next door. She wandered over to our house around dinner not unregularly. She stared through our kitchen window and told me how big my kale salad was for three people. I mixed it by hand, massaging it down. See how small it gets.

Our Santa Monica windows were paned of thin glass; we shared a living room with the block. I'd water the garden and pretend the neighbors hadn't heard last night. As Tony and I failed to make ends meet, fights multiplied. Lots of yelling from me over money. Tony swerved toward the terrain of old lovers. I understood anger born from financial woes. It's immediate family to fear. Tony's onerous harping over my former boyfriends was harder to grasp. He conjured jealous fantasies, of me and my men burning through gluttonous, childless, sex-filled afternoons, not a thought for the rent. But that was never my life. It was Tony's bachelorhood. I'd sit alone on the sofa after we raged, legs pulled toward my chest, imagining his decadence. Tony had made me a mother too soon. Damn.

My bank account was negative dollars. We had separate bank accounts. A thing that once seemed like a good idea; Tony's wages were subject to liens. Time had passed. I became one more creditor. I paid our Santa Monica–size rent and everything else with credit cards in my name alone. I paid one credit card with another. Interest with interest. Debt grew to tens of thousands of dollars.

I anticipated our belongings on the street, a yellow eviction notice taped on our door. I scrambled for work. Sofa salesperson. Art gallery receptionist. Waitress. I'd waited tables to pay my way through college. I always believed I could fall back on restaurants. I'd drop by reservation-only dining rooms and leave my number or a resume. Nobody called me for an interview. When I was a photographer in my twenties, I'd sold photographs in a New York art gallery and taught college photography to make ends meet. But I no longer made pictures; there were no pictures to sell; I was out of date, and thus out of art school teaching. A writer now, with a published memoir, I'd tried and failed to place a new book. I freelanced for magazines. The work was inconsistent and not enough to cover groceries. So I went on the academic job market as a writer, held my breath. Five colleges in the entire country sought a nonfiction professor that year. Hundreds of hopeful applicants applied. A tenure-track job is the academic equivalent of winning the lottery. In desperate straits, I had to at least try.

THE FIRST TIME I saw Morgantown was the eve of a snowstorm. Late February 2015. A clear and cold night. Driving in West Virginia is not driving as we know it in other parts of the country. Driving in West Virginia is like taking a roller-coaster ride through a ghost town. Hairpin turns take you to the edge, even in towns, past husked buildings, suggestions of boom times long ago. Roads hug rural hills. A flick of the wheel or a patch of black ice and you're in the ravine, upside down.

Weather was talked about for days in advance of my interview. Administrative emails volleyed back and forth. Nobody could decide if I'd get there before roads closed. In Upstate New York, Mom taught me to brace tires with chains. Snow was pushed away by plow. West Virginia roads are steep and pothole covered, chewed by coal and gravel trucks. Ice makes them impassable.

A West Virginia University–hired driver picked me up from the Pittsburgh airport. Her long blond hair shined at the crown with graying roots. I saw her before she saw me at baggage claim. Paper written with my last name crinkled beneath her fingers. I introduced myself, thanked her for the ride, and asked if I'd beat the storm. It was long after dinner and not too far from bedtime.

"Just ahead of it." Freezing rain was coming. "The hotel's an hour and thirty from here, a ways from the big city." She bent to pick up my bag, the compact duffle I'd borrowed from Tony. My luggage was beat-up and tied with tattered ribbon; no mistaking it circling baggage carousels. Tony's was travel-worn, but black, expensive way back when. It made a better impression. I grabbed the duffle's handles and hoisted them over my shoulder. "I've got it," I said. "My mother taught me not to pack more than I can carry."

"California to West Virginia?" The driver gave me a long look, ascertaining my sincerity.

"If I'm lucky."

"It's a hard place in winter. Summer, you'll know it's love." The driver placed her hand into her front pants pockets, searched for the car keys. None there. She felt in her back pockets. No keys either.

"Take your time," I said. "I lose things too." We retraced her steps from her car to that moment. "Maybe the keys are in your purse, in a secret pouch?"

She turned her brown leather bag over. Belongings hit the floor. We got down on the carpet together, rifling through old receipts, change, and bent packs of chewing gum. "I guess this is one way to get to know someone." We both laughed, nothing else to do. She hadn't slept for twenty-four hours, driving up and down Interstate 68 day and night, her car filled with academic types or Mylan executives staring at their cell phones.

The driver stood up and gave herself a careful pat down.

There they were, the keys under her sweater, dangling from a belt loop.

We talked the whole way to Morgantown.

It was her first week on the job—don't tell anyone about the keys—she needed the money. Her high school–age daughter had a baby. The little girl cried a lot but was the joy of her life. "She's got such a sweet-smelling head, and the prettiest little fingers I've ever touched." They shared a small apartment. Baby slept in a Pack 'n Play in the living room. Daughter on the sofa. Mom in the master. Daddy was out of the picture. Trouble with meth, he couldn't find work, and he got violent when high. "But there's always time to turn it around. Always time to change. And she loves him."

"I've got a girl too," I said, tired and nervous. I smiled so hard my cheeks hurt. I'd called Jo from the tarmac. It was dinnertime in California. Her little voice. *You coming home before bed, Mama?* "We've got money problems too."

"California?" The driver laughed. "They make it expensive to keep people out."

Brittle nighttime forest whizzed by. "Greyhounds race in Wheeling. You play the numbers?"

One secret Tony keeps are scratchers stowed in his pockets, dozens a week. We never talk about it. I pull his losing tickets out before I do the wash. Each time, it occurs to me you can't fully know a person.

The driver, glancing at pensive me. "We'll take care of you."

We arrived at the Hotel Morgan, where the university put me up. The G in the sign had burned out. The grand brick historic building was named one of the most haunted hotels in the country. It has a full ballroom and a bar in the lobby that looks like a speakeasy. The driver dropped me off at the curb. "See you on the other side." She gripped my shoulders and looked me right in the eye and reminded me how strong I am.

"Get home safe, kiss both of those girls." I squeezed her hands. "Beat the bad weather."

I carried Tony's bag to check-in. The hotel was somber with ornate wallpaper. A clerk behind the counter looked miserable, his head in his hand next to the service bell. I gave him my name and ID. "University bill?" He didn't wait for a response. "You look like a nice person. Don't move here."

PROSPECTIVE TEACHING COLLEAGUES were relaxed and accepting during my interview. Talk about hopes we had for writing work or our children was effortless. I felt an immediate peership. The students were eager, good-humored, talented, and kind. Snow came as predicted. Flecks of white gained momentum before sunrise. It blanketed dirt and jagged rock, the construction site for the would-be Sheetz below my hotel window. A tarp covered a deep hole in the ground, the big basement. I called Tony, though it was night in California. His voice was half-strong, half-awake. "What's it like?" He yawned. "The most beautiful place you've ever seen?"

"Yeah." West Virginia *is* remarkably beautiful, of course, just not from that hotel room window's angle. The university offered me the position a week later. The department chair called. I did a little dance around our Santa Monica living room. The salary was low. It was more than nothing. A lot less than nothing was what we had. The position came with full benefits. A job could give our family a better life, stability for a house of writers.

I took a drive with Tony to talk it over. Jo slept in the back seat. Tony wanted to wait; there'd be other Hollywood jobs for him. Money would come. He had a few projects out for consideration. We'd be all right. The risks of leaving outweighed the risk of staying. "What about culture shock? And medical care? Or schools for Jo?"

I pushed back. It was the same country. Obama was president. Morgantown had art galleries and music venues where left-leaning political groups held rallies and potlucks. We'd enjoy life in an academic bubble. Cost of living would be humane. It didn't occur to me we'd live under red state laws.

Tony parked the car in front of our golden bungalow. He handed me the house keys. I opened the front door. Tony unbuckled Jo and carried her to her room. I walked directly into our bedroom. I called WVU's English department's chair. I accepted their offer. Money could be mine too.

9

Early morning in Santa Monica. A week after I'd decided on the West Virginia job, I unwrapped myself from a tangle of white sheets. Josephine slept cocooned in our comforter. It happened most nights, sometime after the late-shift neighbors arrived home, and before the crickets stopped chirping, Jo stretched across the mattress between Tony and me, elbowing our backs. It was difficult to sleep well with her. It was harder to say no as she pushed her way into bed. Tony and Josephine snored loudly, one on, one off, like a pair of Looney Tunes.

I padded to the kitchen and switched on the coffeepot. Water hissed as it warmed inside the reservoir. I walked down the hallway to the bathroom. I love the morning. I read the news as birds sing *Hello, day*. Our house was blue with dawn and quiet. I placed my hand on the bathroom's doorknob. I twisted it open; a lightning shot traveled from my arm to my belly. I grabbed ahold of my middle. I fell forward and lost consciousness.

I came to with a view: the blur of the white-tiled, ceramic bathroom floor. Josephine stood over me. She'd pulled a kiddie flashlight out of her trunk of dress-up clothes. "Mommy, you sleeping in the bathroom?" She flicked her strobe on, a circle of yellow against my forehead. "You're all right." She knelt close, her breath candied and milk-sour. She dropped her little light. Plastic bounced dryly against the floor.

"Daddy?" I asked her to find Tony. Jo lay down beside me instead.

"I need a hug and kiss." She tucked in. My belly had a crushing pulse. Jo pulled the front of my nightgown down. She placed her cheek against my bare breast. "Fine, Mommy. Fine." Blood pooled beneath my skin, my belly gone black.

"Daddy?" I urged Jo up. "Go."

The two talked in our bedroom; Jo's fearful, small-sounding rasp. Tony's surprised, sleepy panic. Tony lifted me into his arms and carried me to the car. My head dangled over his elbow. His heart drummed against my side. Jo buckled herself into her car seat. Tony and Jo calmly made small talk. I vomited onto our car's floor mat.

Tony sped into the emergency lot. I gathered strength, ran from the car into the hospital. "Labor." I yelled for the

admitting nurse. "It hurts like that." The nurse rushed me
to a bed behind a pleated, pale-green curtain.

I slipped backward into a vast and quiet place. I'd
lost so much blood. I lived far within, like a whisper in a
loud room. "Ectopic pregnancy," I heard. "Ten weeks."
Four units of plasma flowed into me. "Rupture." A nurse
pricked each of my hands, inserted IV ports. Each month
for the last two years, in spite of all the money troubles,
we'd hoped for a sibling for Josephine. I'd desperately
wanted Jo to have one true, everlasting, for-sure companion in this world. Another person in our house.

I implored the doctor to sew my baby into the right place,
her safe home. The doctor was sad on my behalf. Embry-
onic tissue grows inside the fallopian tube until the tube can
no longer contain it. The body bursts and bleeds. There's
no reattaching an embryo into the uterus. Untreated ectopic rupture is 100 percent fatal, for mother and fetus.

Some lawmakers say otherwise. They want doctors
to face murder charges if they refuse to graft an ectopic
pregnancy—a medically impossible surgery. I don't know if
those lawmakers will prevail. But imagine for a moment:
You're a mother with a tubal pregnancy. A lawmaker catches
your ear. You believe. You wait. And that's the end of you.

A NURSE INJECTED morphine into my IV line. It occurred to
me I might die. I would die far from where I was born, and
die like a woman dies, with child.

I prayed beneath the heat of hospital surgical lamps. I was not thinking, *Who will pay our rent? Who will water the star jasmine? What will my mother do when both of her daughters are dead?* I tried reason. *Dear God, please let me see Jo rebel. If I die, she'll discover* Little Women *without me. Dear God, listen: don't you dare do this now.*

Tony waited with Josephine in an adjacent hallway. I called out for him to come.

He carried Jo over his hip. Tony's hair was a swirl on his head, a mess. Tubes and wires connected me to loudly beeping machines. "Mommy?" Josephine stared at my body. "Please." I lifted my head, motioned for them to leave. I couldn't have her remembering this.

I made it out of surgery. I recovered in the hospital for a week. The last day, I floated on a final hit of hospital morphine. Opiates lowered my full voice to a dry whisper, every part of me captured by grief and gated with drug. Tony sat in a chair beside my hospital bed. We argued as I lay there. I hissed at him through clenched teeth, feral with loss. We had no money, no home, no knowable future. It didn't seem to bother him. Our island was swallowed by water. One hundred and ten pounds and I held all of us in my arms while balancing on one foot upon the last bit of unsunk land. I don't remember what Tony said. An unspeakably mean, straight-to-the-heart lie only a spouse can conjure. "You're___. You're___. You're___."

There was no *me* in *you're.* Yet I believed Tony.

Gravity took me down to the bed, down to the bottom.

Our fight ended and Tony left. He was gone a few minutes. I swore under my breath at myself. Where to put
the anger, but back inside? A nurse knocked lightly at the
door. I called him in. He'd been listening from the hallway. Maybe my husband couldn't take care of me, he said.
It was okay to say it wasn't safe to go home with Tony. I
shook my head. Arguing was our secret. Tony made our
meals. Tony spooned me each night. Inside painkillers, I
didn't know what was real. I told the nurse how I'd angered
my husband. I was forcing us to move to West Virginia.

The nurse shrugged. "Never mind."

Two weeks later, Tony and I returned to the surgeon.
He'd pull the stitches from my healing wound. I'd survived those weeks on a steady diet of painkillers and had
barely gotten out of bed.

"And who is this?" The surgeon ushered me into the
exam room. "A mommy-to-be?"

He didn't recognize me. The previous week, I'd made
it out onto Montana Avenue, the shopping district in walking distance from our house. I'd retreated into a salon. My
mother had insisted on giving me money for a haircut,
though on a strict budget herself. I told the stylist to cut
my waist-length hair into a pixie-like bob. The new style
gave me the feeling I possessed the power of a man. As a
man, I had better things to do than grieve a baby no larger
than a kidney bean.

I wept, a humiliation, but the postpartum hormones had me. I wanted my baby, wanted to be that expectant mother. Tony wasn't moved to tears; the photographs of newborns that covered the walls of the doctor's office didn't slice him. I was just a woman, after all, with a mannish hairstyle.

The surgeon stood over me. He'd left the door open. The back of my head was visible from the hallway, my triangle of knees.

"Close the door," I said, a little too loudly. A word I hate is *cunt*. It has a sharp, stabbing sound. But on the doctor's table, that's what I felt I had, a body reduced to slurs.

The doctor spread my legs, barely looked. "Healing well," he said. "We're all set."

Yet he'd forgotten to snip the stitch, the black thread closing my belly button. "Finish," I commanded, pointing at the forgotten suture.

I thought the ectopic an omen, proof of my right choice to end our California time. Tony, who doesn't believe in portents, said it was a sign to stay.

10

We packed our Santa Monica house in May and moved all we owned to Morgantown. We left close friends. We left the stucco-front house. We left a glorious bed of snapdragons outside the kitchen window. We left the fragrant eucalyptus. We left the farmers markets: the strawberries, the dirt-covered garlic, the blueberries black enough to eat. We left the too-green greenery—it's hard to know what to do with a garden that never dies—it rained once that year. It hurt, what I put behind us. There was the wanted baby we didn't have. There was Tony's too-slow-to-build TV career. There was the faith I'd had in Tony as a provider. There was the image he'd made of his own failure, and thus his perceived worth to me.

Tony carried the last of our boxes out. He forced them

into a slim space in the U-Pack. A driver came to pick it up. We sat on the curb and watched the truck leave. It was all gone. Tony walked to the empty house. The light inside cut the living room in half, like folded white paper on an ebony table. Tony was sore from lifting, dusty with cardboard. I couldn't do as much of the moving work as I wanted. My body ached from the ectopic surgery. There was a scream trapped in me. I couldn't let it go. I'd scared Jo and I'd scared myself—we both needed assurance that I wasn't temporary. Jo danced back and forth in front of our bungalow's picture window. It was safe to leave her outside in the small patch of grass we could see.

I stood on my tiptoes and hugged Tony. His shirt was damp and musky. "We can always come back." I tilted my head to the side and up, a chin view. We both knew. We might return. Never again with our trust in one another.

Josephine and I flew to Albany, stayed with my mother while Tony drove the car across the country. Jo looked at pictures of the new house, images online from the real estate posting. "I want the room with the fireplace," she hounded. But every room had a fireplace! Five hearths in the house, all with faux-coal baskets set behind glass. Each bedroom was transferred from wood-burning into gas flame.

The landlord had wanted to sell. His asking price was obscenely high—he'd lost years restoring the house by hand, wanted some time investment back. There were no

buyers. "Romancing a house is expensive," he'd say. There
was no driveway. Not much of a yard. The house was so
near to others it felt pressed against them.

But we'd found a nice place. And it was near impossible
to find a decent rental in Morgantown. Most of the rent-
als were single-family homes transitioned into boarding
houses, places for students. Profits were high. Upkeep low.
Carpets were stale-beer soaked. Wood-paneled walls tack-
holed. Caulk, linoleum, and paint peeled. Asking rate was
around eight hundred dollars a room, pricing out renting
families. It's cheaper to buy. We were in no position to
do so, obviously. I thought it would get easier somehow.
While I steadied us with my university job, Tony would
write another book or sell another screenplay. We'd pay
debt down. We'd get to own too.

Jo and I passed the time at Mom's, fantasizing our new
life. We planned a backyard garden in the little stretch of
dirt behind the new house; there, we'd dig and till and plant
cherry tomatoes. We made maps of the rooms where our
furniture would go. We missed Daddy. I asked Jo to close
her eyes. Remember. I placed her hand over her heartbeat. "You feel that? Daddy lives there too." Tony slept in
a motel in a far-off city called Tulsa. Jo pushed against me,
her chest to mine, in my childhood room.

In our Toyota Prius, Tony was hauling my California
garden: a potted Meyer lemon tree, star jasmine, and a
geranium, an annual I'd kept indoors for a decade, a gift
given to me when Cara died, a promise I made to stay alive.

Tony doesn't share my affection for plants, but he traveled thousands of miles, our Prius a greenhouse: flowers, fruits, and vines dragged in and out of motels. He drove all night the last stretch to West Virginia, right through Kentucky's mountains at sunrise, beating us to the house.

Jo and Mom and I took the route from New York through Pennsylvania and into western Maryland. As you make passage into West Virginia from western Maryland or up from Virginia, you drive over peak after peak. There's the feeling of being swallowed as you go—as if you can't turn back, the same way you can't relive yesterday. Where you are headed and where you've come from are indistinguishable. The view is such a miracle you don't mind that you might never leave. There are fewer people. Rest stops dwindle. There is a convergence of the hideous and the divine. The mountain is an embrace, and all those houses are in briar tangles and the view is vast and you know you are in God's hands because the hills don't end and the fog is the dividing line between the earth and the afterlife.

We pulled into town at dusk, the second week of June, grasses lit with fireflies. Tony waited on our empty porch. Mom and I took a right down South Walnut Street, one made of hand-laid brick. I parked Mom's white Civic at the dead end, our new house on the left. Tony hobbled down the porch steps and to Jo's rolled-open window. Tony leaned in. He reached across Jo's lap and unbuckled her. Nine hours strapped in. Jo ran up and down the uneven sidewalk, her arms in the air, screaming. *Freedom.*

But at arrival, I couldn't look at Tony. I couldn't risk his disappointment.

He opened my door and helped me out. "Come here, Mommy." He says the word and I lose my name; it's locked inside an airless dial safe, code misplaced; I love it every time. We kissed. There we were, the three of us. Home. After not long enough, we ended the embrace. Tony turned toward the house, limping.

"What happened?" His ankle was black and blue and swollen to baseball size.

"The geranium," Tony said, a little angry. Three steps in—Tony's first Appalachian steps—he'd twisted his ankle in a hole in our yard, carrying my plant to our porch.

We didn't realize it then. With all the unpacking, and without a primary care physician to call, it took a few days for Tony to see a doctor. His ankle was broken.

WE SLEPT ON the floor of our empty South Walnut Street house that first night. U-Pack would arrive the next day. Water service wasn't connected, a glitch in my scheduling of things that I didn't discover until I turned the faucet and air clunked through the pipes. We showered at a new colleague's place around the corner. I tried to make our empty home comfortable. Tony fell asleep first, on the carpeted third floor of the converted attic, his whole foot swollen and raised on a chair.

I laid out a down comforter and topped it with pillows,

a bed of blankets in the room that would be Josephine's.
She called it camping; just us big girls in the wild. Jo
begged me to stay. It was hard to sleep. I thought about
the heat and humidity of the South as our A/C hummed.
I wondered if the water would be on tomorrow. I thought
of my childhood in North Carolina as my mother slept in
the empty room beside ours in her own hard floor bed.

Mom moved us from Albany to North Carolina when
I was five years old. She ran from her abusive marriage
to my father into her abusive marriage to my stepfather.
That first Carolina summer was wickedly hot. The street
outside our trailer steamed with rain. There, Mom raised
me and Cara in the-please-don't-bother-me-unless-you're-
dying school of child rearing. The seventies and eighties.
We were latchkey, home alone starting in third grade. Mom
taught us how to slot and unslot chain locks. We stood on
stools and peered through peepholes. We let ourselves out.
We ran untamed through woods and parking lots. We ding-
dong ditched. We practiced French kissing on dirt-grimy
palms. We smashed our piggy banks, crossed the highway,
and spent every last dime on sweets. We took chances. We
survived. I'm still here.

Back in Albany by junior high school, all my teenage
life, I argued smugly with Mom about her having raised
her little daughters in such a conservative place. "But the
schools. And the religious values that hurt girls," I'd say.
"You moved us to a place that set us up to fail." And that
was true. By the time we moved back home to New York,

I was several grades behind in learning. Always playing catch-up. Always in remedial classes.

"What else was I supposed to do?" Mom had asked flatly every time I complained. She'd worked tirelessly, pulling double shifts at work, and made ends meet on less than a living wage.

It was difficult to get Jo down in the empty house—this was a big adventure. I sang songs. I told her a Once Upon a Time story from my childhood, the Parravani wilds. "We were just older than you," I whispered. "And Cara and I played a game: Off With the Dingoes. The dingoes ate all the boys," I said, and Jo's mouth fell open. "And next they came for us."

I awoke our first West Virginia morning to blaring sun, back against the floor. The weight and shape of me and Jo parted our makeshift bed, but in the embrace of soft white linens. I was sore and had barely slept, yet I had the feeling of having saved Josephine as she snored beside me. She would be fed, and housed, and warm, and safe. I would take any risk for Jo.

I would kill a person for my daughter if I had to.

11

Our mountain town deepened, slow summer, forests and vines thickening. Fields opened with blue flowers and grew tall with soft grasses. Otherworldly skies ushered evening; sunsets of fiery red from inside clouds. And the rain. Josephine didn't know rain—our California years, the state was in historic drought. West Virginia rain came. Jo ran outside, closed her eyes, and tried to hold water in her hands.

We made West Virginia rituals. Always out and looking. A kid-friendly bar served beer in ice-frosted fishbowls. They covered their dining room's walls with handwritten thank-you notes. Its ceiling was strung with Christmas lights. Tony and Jo learned tennis, batting balls over a net strung across cracked court. Children ate free at Black Bear. They danced to live music on Thursdays. Two pools in town: one with a jungle gym spouting water, the other with tube slides piped underground; scream through pitch-black and shoot into the shallow end.

Tony and I hiked the Allegheny Trail and Laurel Highlands, the earth hemmed with rhododendron. We climbed the banks of the Cheat. We found multitiered waterfalls and swam in freezing plunge pools. Cranesville Swamp trail sits in a frost pocket. The hills and bogs at Cranesville held a chill. The moist, low-dipped grounds ice in spring and summer. Tony stood in front of me in the wilderness, his body a would-be net. We walked Grand Street and imagined life in big old houses. I liked the pink one with the brown spire and stained-glass windows. We toured the towering white house on Wilson, because someone died there, and because I thought they might sell cheap. We got lost on back roads—the fun was in being lost, our music full-blast, my hand on Tony's hand on the gear shift. We sat on our porch and drank cocktails, counting bats that dove through night as if it were water.

Our family was warmly welcomed into the fold, by academics and by families outside of the university community. South Park was lined with sprawling redbrick and white stone historic homes. Houses owned by lawyers, doctors, and promoted professors who'd bought before the last real estate boom. Faculty salaries earned a mortgage then. South Park stretched all the way uphill. The higher up, the more houses were worth. Down the other side was a cemetery and a primary school and a trailer park. Did the park resemble the one from my girlhood? I drove through, to know. The plots were smaller and the homes in better repair. A mother and daughter sat on their small porch and watched me inch by. I thought then that I'd never belonged anywhere, not once my whole life. Always moving, always making new friends, always on the periphery; I rolled down my window and asked which way was out. What I wanted was to stay and talk. I wanted to explain. The mom pointed at the gravel road in front of my car. It was a loop.

If people from the coasts think of West Virginia at all, they think about banjo music, and Trump country, and sad miners, and blown-apart mountains. They think of shanties. But there are progressive activists, live-off-the-land farmers, and a vibrant community of artists. There is substantial wealth and stunning poverty. Mylan Pharmaceuticals is based in Morgantown: think Synthroid, EpiPens, Viagra, Lipitor, birth control, Remdesivir. People in West Virginia live well off old money from coal, and people live even better off new money from fracking.

WE TOURED MORGANTOWN preschools our first summer. Two openings. One Catholic. One Montessori.

A mother-daughter team directed the Montessori school housed in an old factory building on a busy road. Tony and I arrived early at the large, airy space. We sat in child-size chairs and waited for our tour guides, facing three giant rooms and a wall of windows looking out at the brown river. Our guides greeted us. The mother-and-daughter pair proudly showed us their thoughtfully curated classroom. I wondered how the women could afford upkeep for such a large and well-appointed space; tuition was a fraction of lesser preschools in Los Angeles. The Morgantown school smelled like finger paint, dirt from a butterfly terrarium where pupae hung from leaves, and a mixture of hand sanitizer and poopy pants. The walls were bright with construction paper and lined with bookshelves. Four-year-olds read alone in cubby corners. Others stacked wooden blocks or danced costumed in career wear (doctor, astronaut, police officer) in a tent pitched for dress-up.

I was ready to sign. One thing left. I asked to see the playground. The daughter shook her head. There was no playground.

She pointed at the monster complex next door, a rusted steel building painted cream and spewing smoke, a near replica of the planet-destroying factory from Dr. Seuss's *The Lorax*—the university's coal plant, right in what would be the schoolyard. The plant powers WVU, their deal with the devil. How had I not noticed? Because I hadn't wanted to.

TONY STOOD AT Saint Francis's small chapel, staring coldly through the one-way window at first-graders kneeling on industrial carpet before a crucifix. Our tour guide sensed his trepidation. Before he could ask, she emphasized Saint

Francis embraces all faiths. "What about no faith?" Tony said.

"There's no prayer or religious curriculum in preschool," the guide assured. She waved at a wall of drawings of Gandhi. "Second-graders made these in art class." We'd love it here. She promised. Each classroom was meticulously designed; play fruit stands fitted with cash registers, drawers filled with plastic coins. Cots blanketed with sleeping bags. Washable markers and nontoxic paste topped tables.

The library was vast, a place to get lost. In the middle, a reading area below a fifty-foot glass ceiling. I'd never dared imagine myself at such a moneyed school when I was a girl; I didn't even know such a thing existed.

The playground was our last stop. It had candy-colored slides, a little footbridge, and monkey bars with a mountain view. Tony reminded me he'd been an altar boy. Hadn't I always loved the psalms and the Eucharist and the Holy Orders?

TRUCKS CART FLY ash (a substance more radioactive than nuclear waste) from the university's energy plant. They pull away, snake through town, then onto the highway. WVU sporting events begin with a commercial: a short movie with miners in the hole, helmet lamps illuminating their way through casket-width hollows. The slogan at the end plays and people cheer: "Coal keeps the lights on."

I'd read about the ash online, in an article about water contamination near waste sites. Nobody in my real life talked about the ash. Tony and I debated whether to worry. None of our friends seemed concerned. Was it even a thing?

A humid July night our first summer in Morgantown, Tony drank draft at a tavern down the street from our house, a place with homebrew takeout in amber jugs. The owner had set up shop in his carriage garage. The door pulled up and into a tap house. An un-uniformed man sat one seat over from Tony. He had a truck, he said, a haul from the plant. Did Tony want to see?

The man from the bar and Tony ambled out into the beer-beautiful night. There she was at the curb, a truck full of fly ash. The two stared at the sheet-thin tarp strung loosely over, wind whipping. "You got kids?" the man asked. They didn't share another word after.

Our good friends Mona and Phil live alongside the avocado-colored water of the Monongahela River, in a yellow Victorian less than twenty-five feet from a coal train. It was an early fall afternoon when the freight whistle blew. Mona yelled for the children to gather. The tracks sang, a high ringing of wheels. Jo was shirtless, a pair of binoculars hanging around her neck. She wore green leggings the color of flower stems, and too-big borrowed hot-pink galoshes, to stomp the chicken shit. Mona's girls had had her trouncing through the coop, chasing the hens, hiding in the bamboo Mona grew by the river, and drowning bugs in the deep and narrow koi pond that opened like a gash in the earth. We want our children to hold innocence, to remain young for as long as possible. We'd moved because we were broke. Yet in the move, Jo received the gift of rough country, turning stones with sticks, her face smudged with dirt.

The train's whistle pierced the air, a second warning. Then big black steel rolled in, shaking the hillside as if it had been struck by gods. Jo reached for me like a cat up a tree in the rain, her eyes round with panic, her hair blown back from her face with train speed. She yelled something impossible to decipher. I covered her ears. Mona's house shook—ceiling lamps and window panes and dishes in the cabinets.

Nobody stopped talking. Nobody put their drinks down.

12

Our first holiday season in Morgantown, I still desperately hoped to make a sibling for Jo. Tony was on the fence about a second; one child is easier. I didn't want to listen. After the nearly fatal ectopic pregnancy in Santa Monica, I'd had two miscarriages in Morgantown. The last one, the week of Thanksgiving. We'd brought a puppy into our family to relieve the ache after. The little brindle Boston terrier Jo named Kingsley. We got him from a breeder who rescued Bostons in Freedom, Pennsylvania. Tony scraped together hundreds of dollars for Kingsley somehow. For Jo, no sister; a dog, instead. Our little puppy soiled the house, chewed cords and shoes, and whimpered when left alone. This was easier than a baby? But we loved our pup. And we took him everywhere we went.

It was the second week of December. I was still bleeding from pregnancy loss. Still grief-stricken. Tony had gone to New York for work. I was lonely without him, struggling to keep up with a preschooler and an untrained puppy, but I found happiness in that somber time too. Our girl and her dog. Those two faces. It was impossible to ignore the joy they brought. The night Tony flew home, I drove the hour and a half to the Pittsburgh airport to retrieve him, looking forward. Little Kingsley stretched over Jo's lap in the back seat. He poked his head between her arm and car seat. A line of fur over Jo's legs, like a mink stole.

I met Tony at the arrivals curb. Traffic moved at a clip all around. He hurried into the passenger's seat. Jo waved hello to Daddy with Kingsley's paw. I can count on fingers and toes the number of times I've been the driver with Tony in the car. He's what you might call aggressive: passing often on the left. Pedaling a speed ten over the limit. Leads a lane without fear.

Me, I'm cautious. Granny-like.

I drove south on Interstate 68. Tony gripped the door. He pushed his foot against an imaginary brake on the floor mat; that'll save him. "Snail-paced doesn't mean safe," Tony reminded me, and I reminded him how many times he'd crashed the car.

We drove into Morgantown just after dinnertime. I took a left toward the suburb of Westover: Fairmont Road, past a pawnshop and Family Dollar. The course twisted between leaf-naked, wind-tipped trees. A half-moon was risen. Far-reaching night, the earth seemed lit silver from the inside with cold.

Traffic slowed to a stop. Cars lined the road. Taillights winked red all the way down one hill and up another. If there was an alternate route, I couldn't find it. I didn't yet know the way. We waited and waited. I assumed the jam was sporting-event related. People in other places blame traffic on weather or the rush hour. Morgantown blames basketball. A pickup with a prolifically spewing tailpipe and a decal of a Confederate flag stuck over the cab's window inched in front of us. Tony had had leisurely late dinners with New York friends we both missed, vacationing in our old life. He followed the truck with his eyes, up and down the Dixie sticker.

Jo belted a holiday tune she'd learned at Saint Francis. Headlights from the opposite lane slowly scrolled over us, one car at a time, Jo's eyes icy clear in low beams. The song was a version of "O Christmas Tree," but with a candy cane.

I smiled at Tony. See? It's not all bad.

Jo sang of peppermint-sweet red-and-white ribbons, a shepherd's crook, but on rounds, the opening line again and again. "O Candy Cane! O Candy Cane!" Jo struggled to remember the verses, her voice back there, breathlessly minor and weighted and off pitch. Three times around and Jo got her bearings and the candy song turned a corner. Jo sang brightly as she recovered the words. *Red is for the blood he shed. White is what our hearts become.* Tony stared at me, tight-lipped. *You. You did this. Your choice.*

He wasn't entirely wrong.

Time passed. A half an hour or more. Jo now slumped asleep in her seat, chin on chest, folded in, birdlike. Kingsley curled in Jo's lap. The world in front of the car had grown distant, pinched and pulled like a funhouse mirror's reflection. Me. I did this. My choice. Mercy. I wanted to beg my husband for mercy.

It was our turn at the front of the line. A police officer waved cars along. A wide spotlight tipped skyward behind him. A fire burned on the passing lane's pull-off, hemmed in by a circle of smooth stones. Flames licked the night sky, higher than the tallest man I know. A megachurch stretched down hill from the fire. A little sign planted into the ground: TONIGHT! LIVE NATIVITY SCENE! BETHLEHEM IN MORGANTOWN!

I'd never heard of such a thing. But it is a thing. A fear-fantasy vignette. The show that delivers grace by scaring the hell out of people.

Kingdom Evangelical had propped up a cardboard-constructed inn on a flat off the well-traveled road, beside a painted-green cardboard palm tree. "Paradise in Morgantown." The innkeeper stood inside the lodge, yelling through a knife-cut rectangular window. The word *INN* scrawled in pointy letters across the top, in what appeared to be thick black Sharpie. Joseph paced a few feet away, aware of his uselessness. A heavily pregnant Mary clutched her belly; in deep, unrelenting labor, nowhere to go, no safe place to birth. She crawled on her hands and knees by the fire pit, weeping for shelter.

I WATCHED A reel of the nativity night on the local news, a tidy public-interest story. There was no roadside clip on television. No crying Mary. No fire or shouting or evicting. A lie by omission. The news crew had taken the left past the holy virgin, down the church's driveway. There they'd filmed families strolling a gentle reenactment of the night Christ was born. There were children bundled in snow-suits and hand-feeding llamas, fitting their fists through squares in wire fences. They stroked velvety pony snouts bridled in red. There were bread makers, and basket weav-ers, and boys cloaked in brown robes, waving cardboard swords. An actress playing an angel turned upon the one-story church's roof. The woman in white held her hands clasped at her waist, watching straight-faced, turning, turning. Didn't she get dizzy up there? A halo sprouted from a rod at her collar, up over her head and into a circle woven of tinsel.

From our view, that airport night, drivers stopped their cars, honked their horns, and pointed their cell phones out their windows. I pulled alongside the crying virgin. Tony and I stared at each other in disbelief. We didn't know we could turn left and cruise down to the petting zoo at Bible land. Kingdom Evangelical could teach us the lesson of the unrepentant sinner, and protect our children from unimaginable suffering on earth and damnation in the afterlife. Or not.

Taking a photograph seemed crude; I'd wrong Mary with a picture. I put the car in park. I rolled my window halfway down, gripping the glass lip. Mary took a break from tears, turned car-ward. She smiled brightly and waved, a friend, in recognition.

13

Our first March in Morgantown, a bitter moonless night. Iris was brand new in me. My little bud inside. It was too early to tell anyone but friends. Caroline invited me over for dinner to "feed the baby." I reclined on her plush fainting sofa, in a room welcoming with candlelight. Hers was a single woman's house. A childless house. A space offering a rare and quiet decadence. I'd come over often. Stay as late as possible; time like the freedom of a drug. Caroline had fine china shelved within preschoolers' arm's reach, kitchen cabinets without safety latches, and a prolifically stocked bar; rows of liquor and deep-sweet port.

We talked all night. About Caroline's father's death, playing the job market safe, and what we want compared to what we need. Caroline and I had started teaching at the same time. We moved through West Virginia like dancers learning steps, turning in equal time with worry and enchantment, trial and error. We were better than friends, almost family. Josephine called Caroline "Aunt." Caroline taught Jo to fold a napkin, boil broth, and interpret bits of Shakespeare: *fitchew, twiggin, mickle.*

Caroline and I had made a pact: never move away without the other. Caroline did leave, of course, at the end of our first year. Back to Nashville. I didn't blame her. Faculty of color were few in our department.

"Should I choose a boring husband?" Caroline sat on the floor beside the sofa, her arm propped near my leg, staring at me as if she believed I knew. Should it be a safe partner or a wild one, a man who put Caroline's brain in her crotch? I listed all the enticing boyfriends I'd had in my twenties and early thirties. The one too old for me. The one too handsome. The one too drunk, who'd climbed into my car's open trunk and fell asleep in my driveway. Caroline pouted playfully. "Damn." She laughed with me. "But look at how perfectly your love life turned out."

"Yeah." I couldn't disappoint her with the truth. I changed the subject. "A funny story." I pointed to my belly. "About this one."

Six weeks before, a doctor showed me scans of my uterus. A yolk sac and a fetal pole grew inside. I'd sat in their office twice before, gaunt and defeated. A belly full of death. No heartbeat. Nothing. "What if this baby has something wrong too?" I asked. "An abnormality that requires termination?" I was older. Age comes with risk.

The doctor stiffened, visibly annoyed at my asking. "That won't happen," they said. "God won't allow it."

It was a moment like a vision test, the optometrist flicks lenses: *See this? This? This?* Christian rock piped through a radio in the ceiling. King James Bibles, not magazines, slotted into a carousel by the door. There was a drawing on the wall beside a crucifix, a rendering of anatomy, a woman's slope, tender pink inside. A uterus like a hill to climb.

It had never occurred to me that a doctor would lie. Or religious belief might interfere with patient care. But they do, and it does. Fifteen percent of American hospitals are Catholic affiliated. They treat based on bishops' directives.

Caroline and I laughed uncomfortably about my encounter with the Catholic OBGYN. "Girl," she said, "why has it taken six weeks for you to mention this doctor? I hope you fired them?" I nodded.

Caroline sipped red wine. I drank water. We imagined her future babies. What would they look like and who would they be? Two was the minimum. I didn't have the heart to tell her how hard it could be; you lose family and you do what you need to create your own. I shifted on her pillow-filled sofa, imagining what it would feel like to be able to read all day, or write. Motherhood hadn't stopped me from wanting to get words out.

Caroline wanted to walk me home after dinner. Mothers-to-be need looking after. "I'll be okay," I told her.

"Please stay warm." I'd fare better alone, be safer. There were risks for Caroline. The Proud Boys; we never talked about them. A neofascist, male-only organization that frequently pins flyers up in downtown Morgantown, papers cars with pamphlets, and leaves racist materials in support of the KKK on South Park porches.

"The bridge," Caroline said. "Just don't go that way this time. Okay?"

"I'll be fine," I said. "I'll take upper Park Street."

We'd both been warned not to walk by the Walnut Street Bridge after sunset. Two bridges connect South Park and downtown, the Walnut and Pleasant Street bridges. They're majestic, stone-arched, and stretch over Deckers Creek. Walnut Street Bridge was walking distance from our house; beneath it, people sleep heroin's slack sleep, on the ground or on rain-wet mattresses. Addicts shuffle over the Walnut Bridge, day and night, and around dealers like zombies, their pupils pin-size. West Virginia has the highest number of opioid deaths in the country, a national headline. Heroin is cheap, mostly peddled by out-of-town dealers. I'll never be smug about how users arrive at any bridge; anyone can wind up high. How vulnerable we all are. The Walnut Street Bridge offered the fastest route home. Most faculty avoid it. But that's the route I always took. I took it out of a kind of responsibility: I felt I should be able to.

———

MID-OCTOBER 2001. CARA ran her dog in the woods, down by the Connecticut River. Tents pitched the river's bank, a small city of people down on their luck.

A man approached Cara on the path. He carried a stick, held it over his head, and brought the stick down, cracking Cara's skull. He dragged Cara onto a secluded path. He smashed her teeth. He tore her clothes. He held a broken bottle to her throat. He used her body until she felt it no longer belonged to her. In the wake of the rape and all it cost her, Cara suffered crippling anxiety and depression. She was rage filled. She turned that rage inward.

I wrote an entire book about grieving Cara. What is one girl without the other; half of who she might be. My loss was packaged and published into something past tense—a thing with a beginning, middle, and end; sisterhood, life-exploding trauma, a new chance. I gave the world a book. I lost some privacy.

Now I know a story never ends. It changes shape.

In the last days of Cara's life, five years after she was raped, we weren't speaking. I caught her shooting heroin in my bathroom. I asked her to leave. On the morning she died, seven days later, I woke with a feeling of terrible remorse. I'd abandoned my sister. I'd left her thinking I didn't want her in my life. All I ever wanted was for the sober her to come back to me.

I dialed Cara's number right after breakfast. She didn't answer. I kept calling. I called more than thirty times. She never answered. She was already gone.

Readers often ask me what I think would've happened to Cara had the rape never happened. Do they want to hear that regardless of the attack, Cara would have died? Nobody wants to believe they might also stand on the blade between sanity and madness, or that one event can tip fate. I tell them what I believe: I imagine if Cara hadn't been raped, she'd be a married mother living in suburbia now. That's what *she* most wanted, to be able to choose those things.

What happened to her was a matter of place and time. Sometimes I thought she bore some responsibility for the attack by having been in those unsafe woods in the first place.

CAROLINE STOOD AT the end of her street, waved goodbye. West Virginia wind rattled tree branches overhead like bones. Street lamps flickered, bulbs going or gone. I wore a ratty secondhand, decade-old thick black nylon coat with a fur-trimmed hood and boots that clacked.

A small auto shop with broken fuel pumps sat on the corner of Park Street and the Pleasant Street Bridge. The halfway point home. The lot wrapped around. It sloped creekways. A chain-link fence separated woodlands and pavement. The shop's owner repaired and sold junk cars. Fenders torn off and bodies rusted through.

Five men were horsing around a sedan. They pivoted on and off its bumpers. Streetlamps held them in light,

like actors on a stage. Winter is mostly quiet in Morgantown. Sometimes undergrads set off Roman candles or
firecrackers. Sports fans carry sofas or recliners from living rooms into front yards. They set them ablaze after the
home team wins—upholstered furniture on porches was
banned within city limits for that reason. I always hoped to
catch the deed mid-act. I'd ask, why fire?

At the autobody shop, the sedan's doors hung open.
The men not jumping on the car stood back from it, shoulder to shoulder, on guard. One crawled inside. He cleared
the glove box. Receipts and manuals blew over asphalt.
Another man leaned across the driver's side, rifling through
the middle console. *Don't be afraid*, I told myself. *Remember
to breathe.*

I inched over, stood on the far end of the sidewalk, trying to hide behind nothing. The men didn't see me. They
hadn't heard me coming. I closed my eyes. I remembered
being a girl. Eyes shut and I was invisible. I lowered my
head. I curled my shoulders inward. A porcupine can hoist
her quills when a predator comes. Just keep walking. I told
Baby that nothing bad could happen, my first lie to my
second daughter.

I was half a block past the auto shop. My toe hooked the
raised sidewalk. My body catapulted forward. I landed hard
and with a whimper. Chest down on freezing cement, my
palms and wrists burned. The man in the front seat heard
me, slid out of the sedan, cussing. He asked his friends what
to do now.

I wondered how long it would take Tony to look for me, if it came to that. Jo was asleep. Who would stay with her in the empty house? I picked myself up. I walked at a clip, arms swishing at my sides, casual. I hadn't seen a thing. They were entitled to the car, that's what I would tell them if asked.

The group of five got behind me. One shined a flashlight against my back that cast my legs in long shadow. I walked faster then, more like a run. A house on our block's corner had a motion-triggered floodlight. I took a right onto our street. The light clicked on. Home was six houses down. I didn't dare look back. The footfall behind grew louder and louder. I jammed one hand into my pocket, fingered my house key. It was the sharp thing I had. The cold and running had set me dizzy, as if I'd had too much to drink or sat on a Tilt-A-Whirl. I pulled my long hair frontward over my chest; a cat can pull a mouse back by the tail.

My man was close, closer than I'd realized. He clamped his hand over my shoulder. Squeezed. His palm was large and warm and his fingers were long. The word is *terror*. There's a reason we say "scared stiff." "I'm pregnant," I said. "Don't." I put my right hand over the left, prepared to offer him my wedding rings.

I wear a solitaire white diamond and thin band, Tony's rings. On my right hand I wear Cara's engagement ring, the more modest of the two. The day after she died I put it on. I've yet to take it off.

"Cara?" The man's drawl was slow and sloppy, captured by southern lilt. I heard a voice I knew and I turned toward it. Our jumpy but earnest fifty-something neighbor stood before me holding his hands on his hips, staring at me like a problem that needed solving. Lance was tall and gangly. He's tanned even in winter. He lived a few houses away. Always out gardening, power-washing, or hammering. He held a child's innocence and need to please. Lance was untamed—ethereal and edgy, social and remote, ever-present—a person who didn't understand the concept of tomorrow.

There wasn't a moment we lived on South Walnut Street that I didn't worry. What if Jo slipped over to Lance's? The yards on our street connected. Lance had shown Tony a revolver he stashed unlocked under his sofa. His house was a series of half-lit hallways and rooms to nowhere, like the Winchester Mystery House. He had lawn games and sweet soda. He'd fitted a handcrafted swing on his magnolia, carved the thick wooden seat with JOSEPHINE.

"You out alone?" Lance asked. "Cara, you okay?" He studied me with genuine concern, unaware of his mistake. "We all were just talking about how great it is to have Tony and Cara living on the block." He pointed toward the four clueless men standing a few feet behind. "We saw you. I thought you oughta know how lucky we feel."

"Cara's not my name."

Lance placed his finger on his cheek. He reeked of booze.

"I'm Christa." Voice betrayed me. I was shrill, uncon-
versationally loud, angry. "My name is Christa."

Lance stepped back. I'd scared him, as he'd frightened
me. "I don't know why I'd ever think such a thing." But
I knew. Late at night in his cavernous house he'd read all
about me online. Once he knew, there was no separating
me and my story. He pushed a giant mound of weed into
my hands. It spilled over my palms and onto the sidewalk.
"My apologies."

I pulled the weed to my chest, cradled it. Bits of green
clung to my coat. I walked slowly home, kept it all in hand.
Tony sat on the floor in front of the television at the back
of the house, watching *Cops*; all of that misery for viewing
pleasure, men shouting at other men to get on the ground.
The room smelled of popcorn, strawberry-scented dolls,
dust, and Play-Doh rubbed into the carpet. I stood over
Tony. My hands were blue from cold. My cheeks red and
ruled black with mascara.

"Here." It was too strange to explain. I dropped my
bounty on the sofa. Snarled bud clung to white linen.
"Thanks be to Cara."

14

Early April flowers pushed through spring-thick Morgantown mud. Tulips. Daffodils. And of course, Irises. I'd grown wide with pregnancy; it was past time to tell. No more hiding. My supervisor would need to find a replacement to teach my autumn courses. I found it confusing, my embarrassment to be pregnant so soon after hire. But there it was. I'd proven a bad bet. "I'm having a second daughter," I told the boss, my sex between us. "Due in October."

There was a long, awkward pause. "I like you," she said. "I like you a lot." And then she asked whether a second pregnancy meant I was quitting my job. I squirreled away the proof that pregnancy was irresponsible. "No," I said. "No." For a second I wondered if it was the cost of childcare that had made her ask. We both knew my wage. The conversation ended there.

Work had been difficult throughout my pregnancy so far. I was exhausted, queasy, and slow. Morning-sick all day, I was ready to sleep before dinner. I sat on our sofa each night after class and read student essays, nodding off. I was so tired by the end of the week, I felt tenderized. But I excelled at every university-required task. I needed to prove I could do it all, even if just to myself.

My mothering, though? It fell short. I had what I'd wanted, what I'd asked for, and I worried I was forcing us all through. I grieved for the together time Jo and I would lose by adding another child to the family. I grieved for the wild Jo I'd lost to Saint Francis. I had taught her how to spit. I had taught her how to dig a hole with her bare hands. I had taught her how to squat to relieve herself in the grass. I had taught her how to growl, and never mind her hair.

I'd undone it all.

Saint Francis demanded order. Jo donned a Catholic school uniform now: tartan jumper, white knee socks, and black patent leather Mary Janes. Her classmates were flawlessly coiffed, their mothers too, a picture of Suncrest or Cheat Lake stay-at-home money. Jo resembled an assembly line–made doll. One girl in a sea of girls wrangled into red plaid, but with a single mistake. Jo's always-unruly waves were not Saint Francis appropriate. For the first time in my life as her mother, I shoehorned her.

The morning I caved, I hurriedly dressed in one of the last work-appropriate things that fit, applied a modest amount of makeup, and spritzed on some perfume. I went downstairs, fixed breakfast, and attempted to comb Jo's hair into submission as she ate. We were running late. Fifteen minutes past time. It wasn't Jo's fault we'd slept through the alarm. I ripped the pink comb through Jo's snarls anyway, a brittle flinch-worthy raking. Jo yelled for me to stop, batted my hand away.

"Get it together," I ordered. Yet I was the one out of control. I picked up Jo out of her chair then, hurried. There was a drive to preschool; I needed to teach within the hour. "I have to work." Work's what puts food on the table. "I don't care if you look like an animal."

"Mommy?" Jo was calm, unfazed. She crunched a last bite of toast in her mouth, her lips butter-shined. "Mommies don't work."

"Where did you hear that?" I was still carrying the comb. I dropped it and it slid under the table. "Mommies work so hard."

"School." Jo tilted her head to the side, thinking through what I'd just said. She didn't believe me. "Your perfume," Jo observed. "You smell like a sinner."

I WAS SCHEDULED to give a keynote at a large literary conference the last week of April. None of my work clothes fit. Buttons on blouses gaped. Pants refused to snap. I flipped through my closet and tried to find a dress suitable for the occasion that would also accommodate my rounding middle. I ripped two as I forced them over my belly. The seams gave. All the others were too short, my girth hiking the hems.

I went out in search of maternity clothes. I looked in each town store, even Target, which had two sportswear items in XL. No retailer in Morgantown carried workwear for mothers-to-be. A clerk in Dress Barn said the last such shop closed years ago. I went home and ordered half a dozen things online. None fit. To say I was bereft over such a thing sounds foolish now, alongside all the other things. But is it? If you can't dress for work, you can't go to work.

In *Aftermath*, Rachel Cusk writes:

I know women with four children and women with no children, divorced women and married women, successful and compromised women, apologetic, ambitious and contented women, women who are unfulfilled or accepting, selfless and frustrated women. And some of them, it is true, are not financially dependent on men. What can I say about the ones that are? That they're usually full-time mothers. And that they live more through their children. That's how it seems to me . . . They decide to stay home for a year or two and even things up a bit, like the cake mixture the recipe tells you to divide between two tins.

The idea of selfless, career-abandoning motherhood as a choice supposes there is a choice to be had. Living vicariously through children is both a cardinal sin of feminism and of good parenting. But what of the convicted innocent prisoner who imagines herself from her cell through the pages of a novel? Do we fault her for not getting out enough? This is not to say motherhood isn't a life-enlarging privilege, or children amount to incarceration. It does mean that working women may want to rethink judgment over staying home. A window is a window.

I HAD TO return those ill-fitting maternity clothes I wanted to have for the conference. I was somewhat relieved to see them go, for the money to be refunded to my credit card. I'd found an old dress from my pregnancy with Jo, and a shirt of Tony's that I could wear with a belt above my bump. I drove to the post office, a taped-closed box of wrong-size clothes filled my passenger's seat. An anti-choice billboard faced the road near my house. The sign stretched over a frame resembling a too-high metal goalpost punching a rectangular hole through the tree line. I think it pictured a dimmed room, a close-up of hands cupped dangerously near a candle's flame. I can't remember the exact image; the billboard went down long ago, rented to a new cause. When I was pregnant with Iris, though, that sign was a spirit shadowing me. I wondered for the first time as I drove whether I'd be able to get an abortion in Morgantown if I needed one. What about my students? Or middle- and high-school-age girls? Did the state like us naked and with child? I wondered—and then, I'm afraid, I forgot about it.

I held those girls in my thoughts for not long enough. I ignored the billboard, like it was a person I didn't wish to hear from, tapping me on the shoulder.

I'd never need an abortion. I was done getting pregnant.

I pushed hard on the gas and raced by the sign.

PART THREE

For a moment there was a catch in the voice of the man talking in the darkness. "I loved her," he said. "I don't claim not to be a fool. I love her yet."

Sherwood Anderson, *Winesburg, Ohio*

15

It was early summer 2016, the start of my second trimester of pregnancy with Iris. Jo was four years old. Tony, hired to write on a not-yet-canceled television show in Los Angeles, had left Morgantown to start his job before my WVU spring semester ended and before my maternity leave began. By the end of May, though, Jo and I joined him in Los Angeles. His TV gig was writing for a series based on a film about abduction: "What I do have are a very particular set of skills," says the family man/government agent to the evil foe. "Skills that make me a nightmare for people like you."

We moved into a small white house a block from the Santa Monica bungalow we'd left when we moved to West Virginia. It had an unusable fireplace, ripped screens in every window, roof rats, termites, and a refrigerator with a broken handle. My friend, a single mother, had leased it years ago, before rents skyrocketed. She and her baby had lived there on their own. Her new partner had invited her to move in with him a few months before Tony got the summer gig. My friend's thinking: hang on to the rental just in case, be cautious as good mothers are; men don't always stand by their promises. The apartment was furnished with all the baby things we'd need.

We held on to my friend's home for her and had a place to stay.

This might sound glamorous. In reality I stockpiled every dime. WVU professors go unpaid during summer. I deposited my last check in late May. We sublet our Morgantown house for less than cost. Tony earned just enough to cover rent in Santa Monica. WVU provided generous paid family-forward parental leave for fall. I could stay home after Iris was born, saving on childcare, and still hold my job. We'd almost break even with our stay, and Tony would have the writing credit on his resume. We hoped this credit would lead to more stable employment for him, make up for a slight bit of further debt. It was a chance worth temporarily pulling up stakes for. A chance for a correction in our marriage. Tony back at work, happy.

We settled in for that time. We tried not to look too far ahead.

The lemon tree in our California backyard blossomed. Jo and I simmered water with sugar and squeezed the fruit.

IN MORGANTOWN, THE whole year we'd lived there, fumes often overtook our neighborhood. A bitter smell, like black licorice or scorched plastic. In California, I couldn't stop thinking about it. I rolled over one night, my growing belly between Tony and me. "What do you think that smell was?" I asked. "From South Park."

"I never think of that place," Tony grumbled and went back to sleep.

But I couldn't stop thinking about it. Maybe the smell was old garbage. Or exhaust. Or sun heating the road. Or the waste plant. For the longest time I didn't want to know, and I never asked. Even today, I don't know what those fumes were.

Pregnant with Iris, my senses heightened, the fumes had seemed inescapable. Josephine played outside one warm winter day. I'd opened our windows for fresh air. Fumes wafted inside the house. I ran out to the front yard and grabbed Jo. Her hair held the scent of fired petroleum. She fought me, kicking and yelling as I struggled to carry her. "Inside," I ordered. Jo turned toward the house, slouched and sulking.

I closed all windows, told Jo to play in her room, and went back outside. Jo stared from our glass-paned door, hands crossed over her chest—*why won't Mom come in already?* I walked the house's perimeter, then up and down the street. Nobody else on our block was out looking for a reason. Whatever *the smell* was.

I went back inside. Jo had not played in her bedroom

as asked. She'd crayoned the white living room walls blue. She wiped the clean floor with a red finger paint–soaked sponge. Kingsley was helplessly dressed in doll's clothes.

If we could smell the fumes, we breathed them. If we breathed them, the rain would take them down. Rain soaks soil, soil moves to water.

There was a feeling then my body wasn't mine. I had no control over what happened to it, and to my babies. We had no choice but to take the water in, and the air too. Maybe small steps would spare the baby growing in me. Never drink from the tap. Swish toothpaste out with filtered water. Filter it all. Then I'd lie in the bathtub with Jo, my belly cresting the surface of our water's silky cradle, skin hot and pink and clean.

NAME A DAUGHTER after a flower, her middle name better be tough. Tony liked "Wolf." Josephine preferred "Raisin Gang." It came to me: "True." Tony was driving. I, in the navigator seat, stared at a tangled, brittle grapevine, blown-up dirt flicking our windshield. "What is harder than truth?" We'd call her True. Iris True.

My first prenatal appointment for Iris in Los Angeles, Dr. Y was concerned. My West Virginia records lacked the recommended screening for spina bifida. The window of time for getting that test had closed. I had no idea why I hadn't received the test. It's a simple blood draw measuring alpha-fetoprotein, which is elevated by the disease for a handful of weeks. Dr. Y assured me spina bifida is rare. Chance was on our side. A special scan of Iris's back would show whether her spine had fused. Dr. Y was nearly certain it had.

The sonography technician worked quietly, clicking and measuring an area that resembled a black bean, white pulsing through, like the view of traffic from an airplane. I didn't dare speak. I barely breathed. There was a heaviness in the room, me and the technician under it. Something was wrong. She didn't need to tell me. The technician finished. She walked me down the hall. Dr. Y would see me again.

There was no spina bifida, but there was something else. Iris's kidney was double size, fluid filled. The tube connecting her kidney and bladder was cut, obstructed, or disconnected; there was no knowing. The forgotten spina bifida test had been an opportunity. This scan revealed what we would have learned later, in the twenty-week scan. Early, we'd keep close watch. If swelling got worse, they'd go in. After she was born, Iris would need nuclear renal scintigraphy to assess kidney function: trace radioactive material would be injected into her bloodstream. A camera and computer would record gamma rays, our newborn daughter glowing inside. She'd need sedation.

One in ten Americans suffer kidney disease—twenty-six million people. West Virginians carry the highest risk of kidney and renal failure in the country; more patients there require dialysis than in any other state per capita.

Meanwhile, mountaintop-coal-removal sites are potentially dangerous to fetal development. Researchers at West Virginia University compared the records of 1.8 million infants in mountaintop-removal areas with the records of infants in non-mountaintop-removal areas. The study revealed chronically low birth weights among the mountaintop babies and "seven types of defects in those newborn children, including circulatory and respiratory, central nervous system, musculoskeletal, gastrointestinal and urogenital defects." West Virginia has the nation's highest levels of drinking water contaminants, eighty-three as of 2018. Crude 4-methylcyclohexanemethanol (MCHM), an industrial solvent used to clean coal, was accidentally released into West Virginia's Elk River in January 2014. Ten thousand gallons of the chemical spilled. Contaminated H_2O flowed to three hundred thousand residents. Damage to the liver or kidneys or to a developing fetus is a primary concern from MCHM.

So we had bad water. But we were also very lucky. Tony's television job came with extraordinary health coverage. And what might have been a medical challenge in West Virginia was routine in Los Angeles. We found a pediatric urologist, one from a list of hundreds who took Tony's insurance. Iris needed care. We could provide her such care. California. Thank you.

We watched Iris's kidney balloon the autumn of 2016, just before the big election when a woman ran against a reality television star. The time was a drumbeat. I know others had a sense of foreboding about the electorate, but I did not. To me, everything seemed possible. As the fall progressed, I did become nagged by doubts of returning to West Virginia with two little daughters, one who'd need specialized care. But this is not a tale of California versus West Virginia. There are more hate groups in California than in any other state. Los Angeles has the lowest rate of homeownership in the country. Los Angeles has the highest rate of poverty in the nation compared to other major US cities. Tens of thousands sleep on city streets; many homeless are war veterans. The rich in Los Angeles have wealth beyond imagination. The poor slump on sidewalks next to valet lots parked with luxury cars.

The Getty fire devoured Westside Los Angeles neighborhoods a few years after Iris was born, whole canyons. Nothing but flame and smoke. Everyone evacuated. Yet housekeepers, gardeners, and nannies reported for work; their bosses hadn't bothered to tell them. The world ablaze, these workers were less afraid of lethal fire than of unpaid days off. They knocked on doors without answer.

As it happened, our tough flower was born in California's fire season. Tony's job had just ended. He'd be home with Iris and me, time we looked forward to. It was mid-October, the Santa Anas blowing warm air over parched hills. The earth smelled like straw and dust. Dr. Y was concerned. My amniotic fluid level was low. Week by week it had dissolved, zero-humidity weather the culprit. We'd need to induce labor for Iris's safety as soon as possible. Dr. Y suggested getting an epidural right away; I was open and ready to birth. I'd endured eight excruciating hours of unmedicated labor with Jo. I vomited and cried, sought the return of my dearest dead ones. I yelled at nurses, feeling chewed to bits by jaws fashioned with metal teeth. But natural birth wisdom says medicated labor increases the odds of a "snowball effect." Stalled dilation. Increased fetal distress. C-section. I'd even heard once that medicated labor is akin to running a marathon with numb feet— you'd just fall down in place, the whole road in front of you. I was willing to hurt for Iris, just as I'd hurt for Jo.

I asked Dr. Y, "If I can't feel, how will I push? And if I can't push hard enough, will my baby get stuck?" Dr. Y assured me an epidural was safe at induction, and I trusted.

AN ANESTHESIOLOGIST PRICKED my back for the epidural. Tony gripped my hand. Needle in and the ache was gone. I lay in bed, staring out a window at dawn-lit Hollywood. Lights dotted the rolling hills; so many people awake in first morning. A big fuss had been made over my room. I'd gotten the one that women argue for, assigned by chance but rumored to fetch a high price. My window held the picture of the Hollywood sign in middle view. Those years we'd lived in California, I'd never been able to find that sign. "Is this where it is?" I'd ask Tony in earnest from time to time.

"Wrong way," he'd tell me. "It's behind us." Now I was

a visitor having a baby, and it was as if they'd pushed the sign out, just for me. Big-screen magic. See what California can do. Tony settled in on the foldout sofa beneath the window. He propped his feet on its armrest. I waited, legs numb, sleepy but ready.

It was afternoon when Dr. Y ruptured my waters. A warm rush and the bed was soaked. Dr. Y turned the epidural down. My legs prickled alive. My womb was heavy with pressure from the baby dropping down. I panted through contractions, little breaths, gathering strength to push. I wondered where my mother was. I don't get to see her often. Albany is hours by plane or car, no matter where I live.

Twenty-three years old when she birthed me, Mom was a child herself. Sometimes I run ahead in life, see my daughters on a delivery table. I wonder if I'll be waiting at the hospital door. Or will I be like Mom, far away, unaware I'm asked for. Was Mom thinking of me the way I thought of her? Children leave home; they never leave you.

Iris crowned. "You've got it. You've got it," Dr. Y praised. One last push and I laughed, baby sliding into Dr. Y's hands. Iris True cried, a high-pitch whine like a whip-crack.

"Come to me, baby girl," I cooed. A nurse placed Iris on my chest. She rooted right away, wet and pressed against me, marsupial-like. Her hair was black and long at the crown. It swept forward, like a toupee.

Iris and I were alone in the hospital her first day. Tony went home to Jo. I made room for Iris in my bed, set her

between my knees. She smelled of soap after her first
bath and grunted lightly as I stroked her head. My baby.
My daughter's sister. *Hello, love.* I swaddled Iris in Jo's
cream-colored receiving blanket printed with lime circles.
I'd saved it for five years, hoping for this day. I held Iris
against my chest. I'd never known such joy and peace, the
two of us.

A pediatrician knuckled the door. It was time for Iris's
newborn exam. Her scheduled renal scan was three weeks
away, but what else might be found? The doctor undressed
her. She looked over all of Iris's pretty parts. Round head.
Chubbed, strong legs. All of her fingers and toes. Iris's eyes
were blue as the sea from sky view; Jo's eyes, Tony's eyes.
The doctor got to Iris's ears, stayed awhile; folds at the top,
like an envelope creased. I showed her my elfin ears; my
mother's ears, my mother's father's ears, and before that,
the people of Malta's ears. I'd noticed right away. Iris had
them. I'd kissed both. Iris's ears were all mine. The pediatrician scribbled a script. "Here," she said. "A referral to
a plastic surgeon. People in Los Angeles like their babies
perfect."

We brought Iris home. That night she cried when I set
her down to sleep in her crib, wouldn't stop. Tony and I
stared at each other in our shade-drawn bedroom. Here
we go again, no sleep, only five years later, as if we'd been
freed and then made to go back to life as POWs. Kingsley
slept on the floor. He pricked his ear: *you've got to be kidding me.*

Tony got up. He changed Iris's diaper and reswaddled her, whispered tenderly. Years we'd waited for this second child, for the sleeplessness. He placed Iris beside me in bed. I turned. Iris suckled to sleep. It was that way for months, Iris between Tony and me, happily captured. Jo camped on a cot of sofa pillows on the floor. Everything slowed. Our family of four. Josephine was sweet on Iris. Iris took to Jo. They were like people sharing their hundredth life together.

Josephine now had a sister, and she also found an imaginary friend. Invisible Girl. Invisible Girl had rainbow hair. She peacefully gardened and baked, an only child. And when Invisible Girl felt lonely—which was all of the time— she misbehaved.

One morning, Iris's dirty diaper contained a nearly inch-long carrot. I hadn't eaten a carrot, I thought. How weird. There'd been a moment, an opportunity. I'd left Iris buckled in her swing. Jo played beside her, blocks scattered over the floor. I pulled Huggies tabs closed, pulled Iris up. The carrot hadn't been dropped into the diaper. It had come out of Iris.

"Josephine!" I shouted, a thing that surprised us both. "Did you feed your sister a carrot?" Josephine shrugged. She'd not fed Iris a carrot, but Invisible Girl had.

Jo could be blasé about Invisible Girl's whereabouts. Wasn't it obvious she'd gone to Paris, or preschool, or Kroger? But sometimes she was despondent that I couldn't see. "There she is, over there!" Jo would point.

We took three-week-old Iris for her renal scan. She'd grown longer and milk-fat and yet, Iris seemed smaller in the scan room, and breakable. Tony held Iris as the nurse administered the sedative, her little leg peeked out from a warming blanket. My husband has seen war's grimmest horrors: bodies strewn, people burned alive by bomb heat. Little baby in his arms, wilting with drug, I don't know if Tony's come back from it.

I stood to the side of the room. *Stay with us.* I prayed to Iris and I prayed to God. *You belong right here.* Our daughter slept. Isotope-laced fluid passed through her, lit her veins white. More than an hour passed and then the scan was over. We gathered sleepy Iris, took her home to bed. I stretched beside her until sundown. The doctor called with results the next morning. We'd need to observe Iris as she grew; she'd need more scans and a careful watch. The gap between her tube and bladder had shortened. Good news. Hopefully, she'd grow out of it. Follow-ups were essential. Keep a good eye. I promised I would.

Now, YEARS LATER, Keats a toddler, Iris's kidney still troubles us. West Virginia water. We drank it. Iris in utero. We'll never know if water was the reason for Iris's underdeveloped ureter. When I was pregnant with Keats, we drank bottled water delivered to our door, an expense that felt necessary.

Baby Iris needed antibiotic medicines to avoid bladder infection. The drugs weakened her tooth enamel. One by one her pearly whites went black. I haven't had a cavity in thirty-five years. Jo has never had a cavity. Iris had seventeen cavities at three years old. A dentist put her under to fill them, a two-hour surgery to end the ache rot had caused. Iris has a mouth full of metal crowns now, a silver-shined smile.

THE COUNTRY LOOKED to West Virginia the November night votes were counted. Donald Trump easily won West Virginia with more than 69 percent of the vote, his largest share of the vote in any state. I clicked between channels. It was the same news on every station. Tony and I sat in our temporary Santa Monica living room and watched CNN turn states red. My heart felt squeezed. I had the sensation of swaying, feet planted on a ledge with no safe side. My candidate had lost. Yes. But it wasn't the losing—I'd lost before. That November night it wasn't Democrats versus Republicans, unfair fiscal policy, or even abortion that concerned me. No. I felt as many Americans felt. We'd allowed swirling darkness passage, opened the box and allowed the beast free.

I'd had the luxury of ignoring broken America. I'd believed our country wiser than Trump, not so easily dazzled by Hollywood. Then hate got permission, lies and lying got permission. Cartoons depicted journalists strung in nooses. White supremacists who run down protesters became "good people." POWs, "cowards."

The previous March, before the vote, Trump had said women seeking abortion should face "punishment." Backlash from the left and right was immediate. Trump had gone too far. He recanted the statement and clarified his stance: doctors, not women, should be held accountable for the moral tragedy of abortion. And politicians went on, as if jailed doctors were an acceptable modification. And we went on too. And then Trump became the first-ever president to march with anti-choice activists.

Neither Tony nor I slept the night Trump won. We didn't say much to one another. We held each other instead. With Tony's arms around me, I was protected and alive, Iris asleep between us. We watched the sun rise. There was no other option; we'd return to West Virginia in December. We needed my income.

My body was stiff, sore with sadness. Lack of sleep set me on edge. I felt frayed, jagged, and jangled.

A graduate student of mine from Morgantown called the morning after the election. Whit, a young man from rural Ohio—a beautiful writer. He told me he'd looked down from his window onto Cobun Avenue near South Walnut Street after the results were final. A long line of people shouted on the street below, raw with anger, marching. "KKK!" Whit heard the students yell. "Trump!" He told me this was the first time in his life he'd ever wanted a gun. Yet he was mistaken. The chanting group was against bigotry. But Whit was so afraid, so convinced.

The truth was the crowd yelled, "No KKK! No Trump!"

People shouting in the night, people on the verge just like Whit was, teetering between rage and anguish, despair and terror, pushing out onto the streets, a collective voice for change. "Fear plays tricks," I told him. He calls every now and again. I tell him the same thing.

Jo was up like it was Christmas Day after election night. She wanted to know all about how "the girl" won. What did she say? Did she wear white? Did the bully hide far away?

"No," I told her. "No." Jo's hair was pillow-snarled at the crown, frizzed and coarse as yarn. The corners of her eyes were dotted yellow with the Sandman's grit. "A girl will win next time," I promised. I wasn't prepared for what came next, my daughter in a ball on the floor, crying. What had I done? I wrapped my arms around Jo and rocked her. Hope. I'd given her hope.

Jo attended a Santa Monica kindergarten walking distance from our house. I strapped Iris into a carrier and held Jo's hand all the way to school. We were ahead of the bell, waiting with all the other parents. It seemed wildly beyond comprehension that a political decision could destroy me. What would change, really? My back twisted with pain, real pain. I wasn't prepared for the day, the image of other mothers and fathers in grief's grip too. It's like not having said goodbye to your dearest one in time. We loved our dead country. We'd been too smug to know to pay respect before.

———

THOSE WEEKS AFTER, I took to watching West Virginia news, but from California, local programs. A WVU news crew followed Milo Yiannopoulos as he tucked through a slim crowd outside the campus center. He'd selected our university for the first stop on his national hate speech tour. A small group of students and faculty met him at the door of the student center, jeering, the face of resistance. His talk went ahead to a room full of interested listeners. Yiannopoulos targeted a liberal faculty member with humiliating reference to his weight, sexuality, and inclusive politics. After, that faculty member was targeted, threatened for months and months. He required a security escort to teach.

My graduate students wrote me letters often, reports from the ground. West Virginia to California; they wanted me to know we'd return to a changed place. The campus had been defaced with swastikas. A monster truck drove up and down Morgantown's streets, a giant Confederate flag hanging over its tailpipe, which backfired like a shotgun. The Proud Boys, more active than ever, pinned more flyers downtown, papered more cars, and put birdseed on front porches. Each wrapped in mesh and tied with a bow—a racist note from the Loyal White Knights tucked inside.

I tried to reassure my students, even the native West Virginians. They'd arrived in a place in history worth writing about. Change is worth the discomfort, I said. We have our words. Make it better. Write it out.

I finished my letters and prepared dinner. Jo pushed up

against the table. Iris slept in her cradle one room over. What was best for my daughters?

In MID-NOVEMBER, IN the waiting room at Iris's first pediatric wellness visit, I was handed a questionnaire. All mothers of infants fill one out, a screening for postnatal depression. I'd never had the baby blues. Nothing resembling sadness in the slow days of newborn care. I didn't know how to answer. The form asked yes or no questions:

1) I have laughed and lived on the bright side of life.
2) I blame myself unnecessarily when things go wrong.
3) I have trouble sleeping.
4) I have been so unhappy that I have been crying.
5) Things have been getting on top of me.

The doctor came in to examine Iris. She asked for the filled-out form. I hadn't done the work. "How do I even answer this?" I laughed. "For baby or for country?"

"You've got your humor," she said. "That's all I need to know."

I walked home from the appointment, my hand against Iris's back in the carrier. Her hair blew all around. I opened the door into our quiet house. I lifted Iris out, laid her in her swing. She stared at me. Her eyes were so blue and clear, not yet story-written. I told myself to remember. My world might feel like it's over. Iris's was just beginning.

We were back in Morgantown by the new year. We brought Iris to a pediatric urologist at the university's medical research center. She was six months old. It had taken four months to secure an appointment. She slept in her car seat at our feet. We were one family in a dozen waiting. Two hours passed. One woman got up, hoisted her toddler on her hip, and left. She'd driven two hours and waited four months for an appointment too. She couldn't miss more time at work. We were called in an hour later. Another thirty minutes passed. The doctor hurried in, apologizing. "I'm well overbooked." He clicked on a computer to look at the image scan of Iris's kidney. "That's what happens when you're the only pediatric urologist in the state."

IRIS'S FIRST BIRTHDAY, I carried a cake topped with a single white candle into our Morgantown yard. Our girl had made it to one. I always think of myself as sharing her with Jo. Sisters are more important than mothers. I relished those two together. I'd given all of myself, my body, so they would have each other.

More than two dozen friends stood around Iris, who watched her cake like a fox tracks prey. Iris's name squiggled illegibly across the cake in pastel pink. *"Happy Birthday"* looped under it in too-sweet red and bled into the cake's whipped white piping. Vanilla, four layers high, with strawberries mixed in whipped cream spread between.

The flavor is a family tradition. It was my first birthday cake, Jo's too. There's a picture of me with my little face pressed into the top. Cara sits in the highchair beside mine, her mouth full.

I couldn't eat Iris's cake that birthday. Not a bite. I had the feeling all the time of being on a roller coaster on the way down. No dry toast or antacids kept the sickness at bay. I couldn't keep anything down. I couldn't cook. Meat frying in a pan set me sick. I was whittled slim, the last of my baby weight gone. I didn't know it was morning sickness. The start of this story.

I set the cake in front of Iris. She wore a cream-colored cotton dress with three tiers trimmed in pale blue. She looked like the cake, and tried to take a swipe. The flame flickered as she tried to decide what to do with it. "Hot," Jo warned, staring at the cake, birthday onlookers behind.

"What are you thinking?" I asked. Iris clicked her tongue against the roof of her mouth in her own chair. I thought I knew.

Jo clapped her hands onto the sides of her cheeks. "She's killing me every day, Mom. Killing me every day." So much for sisters. Jo sneered and pushed Iris back, did the honors herself. *Whoosh.* Make a wish.

16

I used to write dreams down. I don't anymore.

A house in dark woods. Two bedrooms. Two stories. Nothing inside belonged to me. Jo and Iris slept in the master, side by side on a too-tall bed fitted with white linens. Keats and I hid in a closet, quiet in our place, still. Thieves had slid a window screen on the house's first story and climbed right through. It wasn't long before the robbers found us. They marched family together. Jo and Iris remained asleep, beautifully unaware and covered and warm. Keats and I were led to them. And Cara was there too, a surprise. She watched my daughters safe. It was one of those dreams. I tell Cara she's no longer of this world. I lose her all over again.

A year before she was raped, Cara dreamed she murdered Art Garfunkel. Stabbed him and threw him in a hole in the ground.

She buried the body by hand. She woke up screaming; she'd killed the voice of innocence.

"What the hell?" I'd chided. The dream didn't sound scary. I didn't understand why it paralyzed her. What do you think the dream means? I think about it more often than I care to admit.

The thieves stood us shoulder to shoulder. "Undress," they commanded. They'd take turns with a sister. One raped, one spared. Our choice.

I handed Keats to Cara, stepped forward.

Keats gripped her hair. Soft brown wound his fist. Dream turns then. "You can't kill a person twice." Cara bartered with the thieves. "I'm already dead. Already raped. Take me."

Cara drew my son in, kissed his head, eased him back over. "Children need mothers," she said. "Go." She waved me away. "Hold yourself together."

I'D WANTED KEATS born at Cedars in Los Angeles, as Iris had been. There's a season for hiring television writers. Late spring. I'd be ripe and ready with Keats in that season. Tony had screenwriting work here and there, nothing life-changing, but enough to keep his union-generated medical coverage. I'd have maternity leave. Keats would benefit from Cedars' excellent care. We'd return to Morgantown after.

Tony said no. We didn't have the money. We'd budgeted

every penny. Leaving was risky. There was no way to know if he'd land a job.

"Listen," I implored Tony. "What will happen if you *are* staffed and asked to the other side of the country, me heavy with Keats and caring for our daughters on my own?" I put my wager down.

"Television's not happening this year," he said.

And then the call had come, toward third trimester's close, mid-May, too late in pregnancy to travel, and right after our move to a new Morgantown rental. A television job needed Tony in Los Angeles immediately. Five months of work. Tony said he could take it or leave it. "It's up to you," he said. I could barely think. We needed the money more than ever. There still wasn't enough for three children.

Tony sat me down, serious. "This is our way out." He was gentle with me, a thing that happens not often. I wonder if war made him gruff, or was he born with an edge. "Hang on. Have the baby. I'll come get you when Keats is strong enough to fly." I didn't know how to say no. I didn't know if I could say no. A choice with a fixed answer is not a choice.

By the time I fully grasped the idea, Tony was gone.

Sweeping the floors. Hammering nails. Hanging pictures on bare walls. Unpacking boxes. Clearing spiders from cabinets. The girls circled the bracingly cold kiddie pool bare bottomed, spraying each other with a tangled garden hose. The tube crimped. Iris stared at the dry hole. Jo moved the line. Water rushed up Iris's nose. Nine months pregnant in ninety-degree heat, I made a spectacle of myself mowing the lawn. Drivers pulled over, stared. A few tried to stop me. "But I like to," I told them. "I want to." Iris turned slate patio stones over; diamond-shaped brown spots pressed into the tall grass. Jo troweled ground inside the playhouse, searching soil for earthworms. She trapped a few inside a Mason jar, topped the jar with hole-punched foil. Worms lashed clear glass. They flipped and turned and tried to feel their way out.

I was getting to know the new house. The view. The garden flowers. The bluebirds nesting our slip of forest. The smells and quirks and broken things. Most everything was broken. The boiler. The garage door. The drains. The taps. The toilets. The wiring. The gutters. I didn't complain. West Virginia rental law isn't tenant friendly. Make noise and risk the street. The house was more than a house. It was a chance.

The move was my idea, my forcing, really. I'd failed Keats in the old house on South Walnut Street. I'd greeted him with doubt. A loop had played in my head: *I can't afford another child. I'm unworthy of a child. I can't afford another child. I pity this child his mother.* And then: *What can I cut? What can I do without? I,* not *we.* I saved dollar for dollar for a move.

I could switch houses. I could bring Keats home to a place where he was planned.

Ken lived one door down. He sunned himself on his

back deck often, on a lawn chair topped with a green-and-white-striped pillow. Iris and Kingsley stared at Ken from our porch; two faces pressed against the patio's screen. I wondered if Ken could feel them looking, as phantoms watch, a world removed. Ken's daughter deejayed in Paris. He gifted Iris her old picture books. Each imparted a lesson: generosity, humility, compassion. I don't know that I thanked him enough, for the books and for being there. Ken had a life-size bronze sculpture of a bear in his backyard and another of a juggler. Every day I reminded the girls to quit climbing the bear. Ken laughed. "Go ahead. Get the grizzly."

IT WAS A Tuesday afternoon. Iris napped upstairs. Jo rolled toy trains across the kitchen. Tony worked thousands of miles away. I was shaking off the bad morning. Trying to forget how little there was in the pantry for lunch or dinner.

That morning, my belly had bumped the car's steering wheel. I'd cried in the Kroger parking lot, the girls sitting quietly in the back seat. My debit card was declined at the register. We'd used the money I'd saved for summer as a deposit on the least expensive furnished rental we could find in Los Angeles, for later, after the baby. We could all be together. Tony was late to be paid, an administrative error. Thirty-seven weeks along and with two kids at checkout, there wasn't enough money for groceries. As I

stood in line staring at our produce and bread on the con-
veyor belt, I knew so many others had it so much harder
than I did then. But that thought didn't stop the Kroger
cashier from looking through and not at me.

That afternoon the air was thick with summer's promise. I wore slip-on shoes and a blue dress with playing-
card-size pockets sewn below the waist. My body was
huge. The house was so hot. The A/C was out. Had been
out for more than a week. It was hard to think. Everything
slowed. So far along, living was waiting; days rolled into
weeks on middle frequency.

The new landlord was sprawled across our basement's
moldy wall-to-wall carpet. I asked after him. Did he need
water? Food? A fan? I was sorry for the trouble. It was hot-
ter inside than outside. The landlord patiently wrenched
the central cooling unit. I told him how fortunate we
were to live in a house with air. We had a kind of relationship now. He was over so often he felt like a room-
mate. He grew up in the house, one of three children; he
knew how hot June got. He'd fix the A/C. He promised he
wasn't going anywhere. He stared at my belly. "Where's
your husband again?"

A sewage-gas grate near the stairs took the boiler's
leaking water. The hole smelled of minerals and copper
and rotten eggs. Plumbing from street to house was old in
Hopecrest—the neighborhood as auspicious as its name.
I placed a cork pizza stone over our gas grate. I could
trap the odor! A thing as possible as caging an idea. If the

landlord noticed the smell, he didn't say. He'd have to fix that too. Silver pipes ran from ground to ceiling around him, bolts and tools scattered the floor. I tried not to take my frustrations about the heat out on the landlord. We were both hot, both sweating. "Let me know if I can help." I turned to go.

"I don't know that you're the one to offer help, so far in the family way." The landlord laughed. "You got a baby in there or did you swallow a basketball?"

"A boy." I patted my belly. "Who looks like a basketball." We laughed together, at the absurdity of the hot house, and of my size. The mood lightened.

The landlord listened to church songs and sermons on a tiny transistor radio propped on the dryer. I stood stairtop, smiling to myself. All I could see below were feet. The landlord's black sneakers tipped away from each other. He was tall and baby-faced and gentle, ageless, and probably younger than me. My grandmother had a favorite joke. I don't remember how it starts. It ends when the sinner enters the chapel and the church burns.

I closed the basement door on the landlord. Ear against the door, there was clanging. The house was quiet otherwise. The landlord couldn't hear me and I couldn't hear him. I sat down on the kitchen floor with Jo and her trains. Dale and Joanne Thorpe, neighbors down the block, had invited her over. "Put your shoes on," I told Jo. "One of the Thorpe boys is on his way." The boy knocked and Jo flew. She didn't say goodbye. I was unbothered. Goodbye was for permanent parting. I wasn't going anywhere. I prefer the girls come and go without worry, without missing me.

Jo's favorite thing was going to the Thorpes'. They had three sons and an open-door policy. The girls were always there, shooting hoops or playing drums, or running the yard. When Tony started work in Los Angeles, Dale and Joanne had fixed me dinner. "Everything all right?" they asked without asking, a southern art. It looked like Tony had left me, it even felt like he'd left me, but he hadn't left me. Had he left me?

"A WEEK-TO-WEEK POSITION," I lied. "Back on weekends." What I wanted to say: *I might be having the baby on my own.*

Situation spoken, its absurdity was clear. It was a bad plan. I didn't have a middle-of-the-night partner. Sometimes babies come early. Due dates are wrong. I pictured my mattress soaked in bloody waters. I'd pull the girls from their rooms. They'd fight the whole way to the car. Who was I kidding? I couldn't even convince Jo or Iris to dress without arguing. I'd drive us all to delivery. Give the girls a video to watch as I labored? And the logistics of birth seemed a luxury beside what was next. The sure thing. After Keats was born, I'd care for him alone. I chewed and swallowed. I couldn't have dreamed a finer point on my worry over adding a third child to our family.

The Thorpes didn't understand the desperation of our debt. Tony didn't understand the desperation of our debt. I didn't even understand. Television work is well paid because it's sporadic. It's a saver's game, a childless person's game. Ambition's debt is astronomical. The money we owed for the months Tony was out of work could pay four years at Harvard. I'd juggle numbers instead of sleeping at night. And this is the American way, borrowing and bargaining. I'm not alone. It's just that kind of talk isn't neighborly, no matter how much you care for fellow townsfolk, bank accounts are forbidden conversation.

The new house was bone silent. Jo at the Thorpes' and Iris asleep, I waddled down the hall. I eyed the flight leading up to the bedrooms. I'd had a hard time climbing stairs. I couldn't lift my left leg. I'd limped up by leaning against the banister at first. When I could no longer limp, I crawled.

On all fours I went, stair by stair.

I made it on hands and knees to Keats's second-floor room. I gripped his crib. I pulled myself to stand. Clean clothes piled on the floor. I bent over and picked up sleepers and onesies, rowed them inside the dresser. His crib was gray. The sheets were white and polka-dotted in red and green and yellow. A plush gray glider tucked into a corner near the window. I'd bought it for twenty-five dollars from a single mom in the neighborhood, an opioid widow.

I eased myself down. "You," I whispered to Keats, rocking. Our ritual. "This is how I hold you. This is how I love you."

A clunking in the next room, Iris awake. She whacked
hard-faced dolls against white crib bars, chattering to herself. She refused to sleep without her dozen babies. Their
cloth-limp, lunch-bag-brown bodies were flecked with dirt.
Their plastic heads smelled like powder. Iris tossed babies
out one by one onto the old red rug. "Up, dollies." Kingsley scratched at her door. He loved Iris best. Always had. I
put her to sleep and he waited bedside until she drifted off,
his legs poking door-ward. He lay on the bathmat while
Iris washed or peed or brushed her teeth. Those two. Pals.
Like no other.

I stood slowly from the rocker, walked down the hall.
Iris's bedroom was street-facing. White noise whooshed
through the closed door. Turn the switch: Wind. Waterfall. Thunder. Jungle birds. There are so many places new
mothers rarely go. The little box brought the world in,
canned. I pulled the curtains open for Iris. She rubbed
her eyes from sun, blinked like a vampire in daylight. She
reached for me. I held tight as I lifted her, stroked her
smooth, straight hair. This part was tricky. We needed
to get downstairs for lunch. Iris was too small to make
it on her own. I couldn't walk down. I carried Iris to
stair-top and sat on the floor. Iris climbed into my lap.
We scooted one step at a time. It was a game we played.
Song and all.

"One, two, three," I sang. "Four, five, six." We were halfway there. Iris clapped along to step-music. "Seven, eight,

nine." I misjudged the distance, tipping forward. We two rolled, turning one on top of the other, bodies thumping slick wood. I wrapped my body around Iris's as we tumbled, worried for her head. We thudded at the bottom. Splayed on our backs against the ceramic gray foyer. I couldn't get up. I couldn't pull myself up. I was anesthetized by adrenaline. I rolled on my side and ran my hands over my body, checking. Iris sat up, clapped her hands, and laughed. What a ride. "Mommy, do it again!" She toddled around me in the hall, where I curved like a question mark. "Mommy!"

"Jo!" I yelled, forgetting she'd gone. My phone had fallen from my dress's pocket. It lay an arm's length away, the face cracked. A car's engine rumbled in the driveway, the landlord leaving. "Phone," I asked twenty-month-old Iris. She tipped her head to the side and bent her knees, staring at me as if she were looking under something.

"Phone." Iris picked it up and handed it to me.

I dialed New York. "Mom? You were wrong. I can't do it," I cried. "I can't do everything."

"What are you talking about?" Mom asked tensely, small-sounding, a person in a shell. Cara died in the month of June. It's the month Mom can't mother me. Ordinarily, I know not to ask.

Keats's birth, promised on Cara's death day, posed a what-if question. I'd asked my midwife to induce me, to avoid the collision. I was booked for the eleventh, a two-day grace.

"I need you. Mom. Please?"

"I have to mow the lawn," she said. "I have to get my hair cut."

Mom was there to help the day after next. She rang the doorbell early and wished me good morning.

17

I was thirty-nine weeks pregnant when the midwife swept my waters. A week to term, she edged her gloved finger around Keats's amniotic sac and my cervix, separating us like cake batter from a mixing bowl. I was two centimeters open. Membrane sweeps coax a baby ready. There was no harm in trying. This was the best she could do, more effective than waiting. The rest was up to me. Home remedies can work. We didn't speak of them. A mother of two knows. Castor oil. Foot massage. Brisk walks. Fucking.

Call when contractions start.

Tony and I trekked White Park, which wasn't white but green, with twisting hills and poison-ivy-heavy switchbacks. Leaves shimmied overhead with wind, hands waving. I was two steps ahead, maybe farther. Going hard.

"You feel anything?" Tony yelled from behind. *Feeling*. By which he meant pain.

Sweat rolled down my back. I was out of breath. Baby pushed against my lungs. My shins and knees were red, forest slapped. I itched all over. My skin stretched as far as it could go. My breasts were heavy, my nipples rosy targets. Hair stuck wet against my neck. My legs and feet ached. My thighs spasmed, a perpetual charley horse, but everywhere. But I needed to move. Keats needed out of me. Born with a father in the room. What did I feel? What I'd feared I'd feel on the eve of mothering a third child. Crushed. Hopeful. Reduced. In love. Unqualified. Trapped. Hurried. Raw as a picked scab. Abandoned.

Keats hung low, dropped and ready. I could carry him still, fingers looped under belly. "Keep going," I shouted back without looking. No labor yet. I plowed path, overgrown brush sweeping my legs.

Yesterday, I was to be admitted and induced. Yesterday, the hospital was overcrowded; no room. Six days from the hike, Tony would fly again.

We hiked the mile. I was twenty feet ahead now, at least. A pair of women approached on the path, little dogs running as far as retractable leashes would allow. The trail curved, sloped up and downhill. Tony was at a bottom. To see me alone, child-fat and fast-going, I was a surprise. A sasquatch. The women stared at each other, eyes wide with alarm, a look suggesting the question of interfering. I nodded. We three passed without a word.

I walked to the straight, a wood and stone balcony jutting over Deckers Creek, marking trail's end. Tony was right behind. Trees parted the water. The distance revealed pine mountain, rusted building cranes along the Monongahela River, and a Toyota dealership on a busy road. A waterfall flowed below the balcony, slipped beneath rock. It went underground and wove the land, like thread through cloth. Before we moved to West Virginia, I didn't even know such a thing was possible. Mother Earth surprises.

Frothy brown creek overflowed onto the muddy bank. "Now what?" I asked Tony. "Now where? What am I going to do if this doesn't work?"

There was the *I* not *we* again, single pronoun sneaking in. A snitch, a stealth intruder. Tony had lost patience with it. "Stop it with the single-mother fantasies. You're not your mother." Two girls and me in the house alone? I felt like my mother.

Tony was with us. Just gone sometimes.

I knew Tony's line. "Why can't you see?" he would shout. "Morgantown is a dead zone, nothing for children, no future." He refused to go down with the ship. "You think I enjoy this?" But let's be honest, he did enjoy it. Tony missed the girls, but in California he set my calls to silent.

I stopped to rest, heart pounding, my chest tight. I bent over without bending over. My belly was so wide, I couldn't see my toes. You get big and ignore everything below. Creams. Razors. Polish. The baby is born. Your crotch appears, a long-lost friend, only bruised and split like a peach.

I stood in the forest beside Tony, thinking of what I'd do for our babies. I'd fight wild animals. I'd even fight my husband.

We went home and stripped our clothes. The last things that fit me, black and cotton, were twisted into a ball on our bedroom floor. My mother sat in the backyard with the girls. I could hear them yelling. Iris had stolen plastic fruit from the playhouse. She chucked it down a hill, one piece after another.

I'd gotten the playhouse a year ago. It belonged to a family with grown children. They'd given it to me for nothing. Just take it. Solid wood. Hand-built. A one-room cottage with three shuttered windows, shingled roof, and weathered front porch. How I'd longed for a playhouse when I was a girl. I'd spackled this playhouse with sand. I spray-painted white over. The house had tooth. The feel of sandpaper. The look of a California bungalow. I washed the porch a Cape Cod blue.

Tony and I climbed into bed. Sex triggers labor. We made love, but I can't call it love. We made anger and resentment. I straddled Tony, squeezed his freckled shoulders as the force of his body in mine opened me.

After, I showered. Hot water pinked my skin. Steam clouded the bathroom's mirror. Soap slid over my belly and funneled the drain. Filth from White Park all the way down. I placed my chin on my chest. *Come on, baby boy.* I asked my son here. There was a break in me, my body a fault line. I called. Keats answered.

AT THE NURSES' desk, hands cradling my belly, I waited for another wave of pain and signed myself in. Contractions with Keats were light, little more than a twitch, or a balling of a fist. Not the crushing kind I'd had laboring with Jo and Iris.

His labor was like the baby he is: soft.

I asked for all the drugs anyway.

I wasn't sure this was *it*. The body prepares for birth with twinges; cramps come and lead to nothing. I carry strep B, a bacterium naturally occurring in a quarter of pregnant women. A newborn infected at delivery can suffer palsy, death, fever. IV antibiotics are administered for the baby's protection as a precaution. First sign my body is ready, I go. I needed my son safe from sickness in me.

I said a little prayer at check-in that I was far enough along in labor to be admitted. There were few beds open. A nurse walked me down the hall to an exam room. We passed a full-bellied woman who fought to stay. I was seated in a plastic tan recliner in a closet-size room. A technician fitted my waist with a white elastic belt. It connected me to a machine measuring contraction pressure. A print strip eased out, like paper from an old-fashioned tabulating calculator. A graph of scribbled flow, spikes and flats. It was my time. The nurse sent the fighting woman home and gave me her room.

A few hours passed. Now what? Tony and I shared small talk. About his new coworkers. About the still-broken air conditioner. About the clever things Jo says. I asked if he thought Mom could handle the girls alone tonight. "Don't worry about your mother," Tony said. "She's been around longer than either of us."

The midwife checked me every hour or so. She apologized each time for the intrusion, palpating my cervix, eyes northward, thinking. What to do? I hadn't dilated. Labor was stalled. With Jo, freight-train birth. Iris came slow, subtle but insistent. Keats was on his own schedule. Watch him hide. Watch him stay.

The midwife asked a kind-faced brunette nurse to administer a Pitocin drip to get things going. Another clear bag hooked above the birth bed, fluid swirling the IV line. It was right before dinnertime. I don't remember eating. I don't remember being hungry. Maybe Tony went downstairs to the hospital's cafeteria, maybe he didn't. He doesn't remember either. I've asked him, as I ask for his help filling in the details of Keats's birth I don't recall or couldn't see. Tony as observer, second scribe to a story that brings him a certain amount of discomfort.

"What does your husband think?" A question I'm asked. The answer: He's hurt by this story. He thinks it's a book about wishing I'd aborted our son (a thing he says), and therefore a book about not wanting him as a husband (a thing he feels but can't articulate). But neither is true. I see a couple struggling, not connecting, needing to provide for our children. Tony sees his failings reflected. He even gets a little haughty; he's the good father to my bad mother. Below those first feelings, Tony knows he's less important to the story. That hurts.

I REMEMBER THE sunset. The room dappled orange. There was the smell of rubbing alcohol and pine floor cleaner. The sound of voices outside the closed door, people passing. A night storm rolled in; full-on hellcat wind. Rain drummed the windows and roof. I stared out at the black sky and hoped I'd beat the latest hours, a baby in my arms before midnight.

Tony made his bed on the pullout, closed his eyes, folded his hands over his chest. A corpse in wake.

I didn't hurt. I didn't feel. Pain meant progression. Pain was proof. I willed pain. There had been but one way to walk forward these months. It required a kind of numbness, a buffing-out. Labor gives permission to scream.

The cramps came little by little. Their heat spread over me. I turned to Tony and told him what I felt. Fire ants biting skin. The squeeze of sit-ups. I pressed the call button. The midwife returned. She pulled on a glove and commenced her ritual prodding. The sensation of her hand in me had lessened both in intimacy and discomfort.

She could steer me with two fingers held together as if in salute. She was getting me there, closer and closer to Keats. I missed someone I'd never known. I longed for someone I'd never seen. Waiting for your baby is a penetrating homesickness.

An anesthesiologist wheeled in a cart. Tony guided me to sit at the edge of the mattress. He held my hand. I squeezed back hard. Epidural tubing threaded my spine. A pinch as the line snaked. Tony helped me back to bed, his arms around me. Drugs did their work. They unraveled fear one backstitch at a time. I lay drowsy but present. I was content, as if taken by the fireball bliss of whiskey. My legs went numb. I looped my hands under one knee, picked it up, and let it drop against the bed. Dead weight. I was wrapped in peace. We'd be all right.

What happens next could have happened anywhere. It happens more in red states, in places where money is lifted from women's health care. It's not as simple as matching words with meaning on a worksheet by tracing the line, or as $1 + 1 = 2$. And it's not the fault of hard-working doctors, nurses, and midwives. If anything, they're working even harder than they have to. But it's a fool country that does not connect circumstance and outcome. The systems are burdened.

Epidural anesthesia has risks. I took them. You sign and date a form. You're made aware of rare danger. I thought little of it. I'll never know whether choosing an epidural set the next weeks into motion. Maybe not just weeks.

For years I wondered if Cara knew her last hit was the end, if she'd been afraid. If she was ashamed for how bitter she'd been. Had she grieved for life, for what would never be? Like for right now?

That's what the heroin was for. To temper such questions.

BIRTH IS DANGEROUS. A woman having a child today is twice as likely to die in pregnancy, childbirth, or postpartum than her mother was.

And I am at an advantage as a white woman. The United States has the highest maternal mortality rate in the developed world. Black women are at the highest risk of death. Nearly a thousand women of color died from pregnancy-related illness in 2016 alone. The Center for American Progress cites: "African American women are three to four times more likely to die from childbirth than non-Hispanic white women."

AN HOUR AFTER starting epidural anesthesia, my blood pressure plummeted. A frightening but not uncommon side effect. There were telltales: stars flashed around me, like a whack to the head. Bells pealed in my ears. I took leave; the surrender of falling backward into nothing. A pillow over the face. I didn't fight. No time to fight. Nurses rushed around the bed, my body. One pushed adrenaline into my IV line. Back up to the surface, back with the living.

A few minutes later, I was laughing. Twelve years to the day that Cara died. All I could do was laugh. I wasn't dying; Keats was getting born.

A baby arrives when he wants. Sometimes a day is just a day. Sometimes too, a person is unable to manage the weight of the meaning of the thing right in front of her. But what is past without meaning made?

HERE'S THE THING. Cara put the needle in her arm. She kept putting it there. Whether I bathed her in affection. Whether I scorned her self-destruction. Pointing it out didn't kill her. My voice didn't kill her. Heroin killed her. It didn't take twelve years to learn that, but it took me twelve years to learn I punish myself by going too easy on people and places.

So what happens if I don't tell you about the time I couldn't get an abortion, and then my son was born sick? Nothing happens.

And what happens if I tell you about the time I couldn't get an abortion, and then my son was born sick? You tell me.

PART FOUR

We see the flying bird. Sometimes we see
the trace of it. Actually we cannot see the
trace of a flying bird, but sometimes we
feel as if we could.

Shunryū Suzuki

18

I labored with Keats in an overcrowded hospital nestled at the base of West Virginian foothills. Morning's light, the room's window view was green and lush but for a concrete, smoke-spewing, open-mouthed coal stack in the not-too-far-off distance. After fourteen hours, it's "prolonged labor." I was beyond time. Twice the time it took with Jo or Iris, though third deliveries are usually faster. The first baby breaks you, stretches and seasons you. Ten is the destination—the centimeter width the cervix needs. I was a six. Six for hours and hours.

Nurses switched my drained IV fluid bags for full. I was never without antibiotic cocktail. The wall clock ticked: morning. Late morning. Early afternoon. How long before the hospital got antsy and a doctor brandished the knife?

"Please don't section Keats," I petitioned the midwife. I feared caring for three little ones alone after major surgery. The night feedings, and swaddlings, and the stairs. Jo and Iris in need of lunches and baths and tuck-ins. Could I do it all with a belly gash sewn like a football? "Please," I said again. "No."

My midwife nodded. She understood the circumstances. Tony had gone to every prenatal appointment when I was pregnant with Jo. Pregnancy's wonder had worn. This midwife hadn't met Tony until deep in the third trimester. I had the babies. He was elsewhere. I'd told her of his work. A job in California! How shiny.

There was no surprise, no judgment. She's a veteran of West Virginian obstetrics, has seen women struggle. Women with vastly harder lives than mine. "We'll do what we can," she said. "And what's best for baby." She left and soon returned, a foot-long needle hooked at the end in hand. She pricked my waters to move labor along. There was an immediate relief of pressure, a shifting inside. Keats moved into position. I rushed to ten. It was time to push.

I bore down, chin against chest, whole body coiling around contraction. There was delivery's familiar fullness below, my body at capacity. Tony stood to my left and held my leg back. A nurse stood to my right and gripped my calf. The midwife waited between. We went rounds. Count to twelve. Take a breath. Begin again.

"There he is." The midwife's voice broke with potent joy, as if her first time with the miracle. It's a job with long hours. Midwives work nights, weekends, and holidays. Always on the clock, she's at every one of her patients' births. It was the reason I'd sought her care. I didn't want a doctor assigned to labor on rotation. I longed for certainty, for a familiar face. "Go. Go. Go," the midwife commanded. I pushed as hard as I could. There was a burning between my legs, skin tearing as Keats inched forward. Ring of fire. I pushed through heat, crying out from exhaustion. I was so close. *Get here, boy. Let me devour you with love.*

Keats crowned. I reached between my legs and touched him, a patch of baby, head top wide as a navel orange. I'd done the same with Jo and Iris. It helps to feel your kin. Keats's wet hair was silky as underwater grasses. Three more rounds of counting and pushing. "Keep going. Keep going. Don't stop." The midwife readied her hands, parting them for Keats as an open book is held. Keats was faceup, head out to the neck and going nowhere.

The midwife tensed her mouth. Her easy mood vanished. She leaned closer to me. "Push." A short-in-stature woman, stout, with cropped gray hair and wire glasses, she's the kind of person you want to embrace. But she has a strength, like a person who can break a horse with a look. "Push." She squeezed my leg.

I've pieced together a picture of the delivery. Nobody mentioned the emergency. Not then nor after. Tony's uneasy eyes; he hadn't seen this before. An ache in my hips as Tony and the nurse forced my legs back harder. Light in the room; clinical white and still. There was the tenor of a bank robbery.

The teller pretends, sparing workers and patrons anguish, gun pointed at her chest, counting the money. Keats was blue, not baby blue but trouble blue. There was something wrong, clearly wrong. I'd felt what was wrong was me. I wasn't putting in the required work. I was lazy. Out of shape. Numb.

The midwife reached inside me, hand to elbow, and twisted. She pulled Keats down and out. He wasn't born, but ripped from me. Limp and purple, he didn't squall. Tony cut the cord quickly, with purpose. He observed his son with the honor of a war flag. It was written on his face, in the tension of his arms, Tony's fingers tender on Keats's neck. Love and terror.

Touch has a memory.

Tony lost a father and gained a son. The atheist believes.

Tony passed Keats to the mountain midwife and officially into Appalachia.

Nurses whisked Keats away. They worked on his little body, on an exam table away from my eyeshot. "Tell me he's okay," I asked no one. It was minutes or years. In that time, I thought I held the moral of a story: what a shame, a mother who doesn't recognize fortune over failure.

A nurse carried Keats over. I pulled him to my breast, cordless, rubbing him into his voice, skin to skin. We both cried out; him from the shock of life; me from the shock of that life colliding with something close to death. I was greedy with him, with the relief of my son in my arms. I kissed his honey-flesh first, his bud lips, his tiny pink hand curling my pinkie. Keats's back rose and fell, quick breaths. A son occupied less than a hand's width of my chest. The hospital's index-card-length diaper and plastic anklet so big, nearly slipping off. Our middle-size baby. Seven ounces more than Iris, seven less than Jo.

"Remember me?" I stroked his back with feather-weight. "This is how I hold you."

Tony held Keats next, effortlessly cradled him. A natural father. Jo was born and Tony taught me how to support her: Elbow under the neck. Arm like a pouch. Babies are fragile, not broken. Tony carried Keats to the window, talked to him as if talking to an old friend. The two were made to be father and son. A pair for this world.

TONY CALLED MOM that afternoon, Cara's death-day anniversary. "Your grandson is here." Mom arrived within the hour.

She walked to my bed, stared at the babe in the cradle beside. I wondered if she was remembering Cara in her bassinet. Mom sat on the pullout sofa below the window, smiling, her shoulders turned in like a claw. I wanted to ask if she was all right. I was afraid for her answer. She said for the first time in twelve years she felt hope.

And yet we think the greatest pain's to die.

IN THE HOSPITAL, Keats shivered, so I dressed him. A cream cotton gown. Teal-collared and printed with yellow ducks.

The garment was Jo's. Something picked long ago from a bag of hand-me-downs. I lay Keats on the birthing bed. My knees bowed around him. White sun flared the room. Shadow pitched the closed wooden door. Black scuffed the shined floor, rubber of wheels and shoes. I was captured by relief, and suspicious of the feeling, like a happy ending to a brutal war film. The room's walls were painted sage, trimmed in buttercup. Calming shades. Decor of a quaalude.

Mom walked to the bed, a searching look for Keats. "Who are you?" she asked, a question not for Keats but for his trickery. A day of grief swapped. She lost a child. I got a boy born under a Gemini sun. Mom waited for me to answer for Keats. The whole pregnancy Mom joked she wanted a bambino this time, a boy with coal-black eyes and a full head of carob-brown curls. No more blue-eyed blondes like the girls. Her wish granted. Keats has eyes like Mommy's eyes. Eyes like Cara's eyes. His arm, though, it hung there.

Mom held Keats and he cried. He wouldn't stop crying. Yowling like a cat's tail pulled. "I don't think he likes me." Mom frowned, eased him back to me.

"Babies don't know," I snapped. "Maybe he smells the cigarettes." We repel as magnets do. Mothers and daughters. The powerless fighting the powerless.

19

Sun from our hospital room's west-facing window washed Keats gilt-fleshed. Vermeer-like: *Mother Cradles Babe in Sterile, Cluttered Hospital Room.* It was magic hour, that term photographers use for candied-orange dusk. A world cast in perfecting light. Not as we are, but as we wish to be. Softer. Blazing. Touched.

I held my son in golden West Virginia. We were alone. Together yet alone.

Mom and Tony had gone home to be with the girls. Circulated air whirred the hospital room. The tear between my legs from Keats's pulling-out throbbed. He was hungry. I wasn't hungry. I hadn't touched the fat-hardened meat loaf and crusted-over potatoes on my dinner tray. I'd propped pillows. Pushed them against the labor bed's small walnut-colored headboard. I needed a better angle to nurse. Keats hadn't latched. We'd tried for hours and hours.

Exhausted, my boy slept heavy on me. I stayed still as possible, holding his slumber. Venetian blinds swayed above the air-conditioning unit, a light tapping against window glass, like a wall clock ticking in a roadside motel.

I lifted Keats to my breast. I kissed him awake. A peck over each closed eye. I wore a gray robe trimmed with black lace. I was gifted the garment while heavy with Iris. I wore it pilled and stretched and milk-stained. That robe dignified in an otherwise unruly, dreamless time, in the day-dim house, shades drawn to urge Iris into circadian rhythm. I welcomed Keats to the old garment. I tugged open the cotton ribbon bowing the robe together. It fell over the white pillows behind. The air was bracingly cold.

I was bare for Keats, more than bare. I was naked. Nothing on but mesh underwear stacked inside with pads collecting rusty birth blood.

The empty IV port still poked into my hand from labor was covered with soggy medical tape. I struggled to keep Keats's weight from pulling at the needle. I parted his lips with my pinkie, my most nipple-like finger. I slid it between his gums. He clamped down, trying to suck, managing only to bite. He arched his neck and wailed, his arm against his side, body turned toward mine for warmth. Frightened. Keats was so frightened. Hunger was an unknown, a not-yet-solvable sensation. Hunger was an empty bottomless terror. I tried to plug his mouth with my nipple. He spit it out.

A nurse asked after us every couple of hours. Hospital protocol: How long a feed? Which breast? Was the other offered? I couldn't answer. Keats's situation was unclear. He wanted the breast. He seemed to know it was his. His mouth worked against him. He'd come on and release. I learned to avoid calling the nurse into the room when I needed her, to avoid those questions.

I pulled Keats away from me again and again. I tipped his head back and then quickly up, his lips puckering by instinct. I thrust him onto me. A jamming of infant to nipple. I knew how from birthing books, as La Leche would have it. The unpracticed nurser might think this move a kind of violence. It's a maneuver like a molly takes her kitten to jaw, that painful-looking hanging from the neck that is actually loving pacification. But Keats didn't fit me. I wasn't the right shape.

Early hours post-birth had been a forgiving time for me before. A trust-building time. There's no milk directly following birth. Milk comes at home, a rush of fluid with the force of fire. Those first hours, a newborn takes in mere drops of colostrum—greasy and yellow, nourishing with near nothing. A whisper of milk, a suggestion. I squeezed colostrum onto my fingers and rolled it over Keats's tongue. He would have from me what he couldn't take on his own.

Breastfeeding is a collaborative dance; new partners learn the groove of their paired bodies. We only needed to be together. We'd adjust: A mouth not opening wide enough. A cradle-hold too loose. One of us too tired, too hungry, too frail. It had always worked before. We didn't need to be perfect. I tried to remain optimistic.

Jo had had a strong latch. Iris too, though she'd rooted gently, as if asking permission. My nipples cracked with both girls; crescent-moon-shaped sores scabbed where their gums met my flesh. The wounds healed. The girls grew fat. I was able to ignore the thought of my blood in their mouths. I'd mothered with the luxury of easily latching babies.

Keats seemed sleepy and stung. He cried more than the girls had. He flinched when held. One of his legs shook incessantly, a muscle stutter, an over-and-over-again twitch. He was so like the girls in other ways. Good weight and tone. Body long and lean. His cobalt eyes clean as an untouched canvas, deep with potential.

Mothers learn a baby's cry. The special meaning of each wail. A triangle chimed from opposite angles. I thought I knew them all: Wet diaper. Too hot. Too cold. Lonely. Hungry. Over-full.

But pain. I didn't know pain's sound. Not like this.

"Keats, baby." I was soft. "Show me how to make it stop." He had no answer, of course. He was the one asking me.

The moment I'd been waiting for. I was failing him in our short hours.

I RANG THE call button. The yellow help light blinked like a traffic caution. A nurse on her way.

After an hour of trying to feed Keats, I was hungry. I needed to pee. I needed washing. I can't do this, I thought. I stared at a poster print of a meadow landscape framed and hung on my hospital room's wall. I looked through the picture and not at it instead of staring at the real green earth outside.

A few hours before, in the blissed calm after Keats was born—Tony asleep on the pullout, Keats asleep in his bassinet—I'd rolled over and lifted my legs to sit at the side of the bed and eased my feet onto the cold floor. *I can get up on my own,* I thought. *Tony's tired, don't ask.* But my body didn't hold. I slipped to the floor like a person without bones. And quietly. Neither Tony nor Keats woke, a thing I held as a mark of success, excellent mothering, and generous partnering. Legs pulled open like a wishbone only hours before, birthing had pushed my pelvic bones too far apart. Yet it barely fazed me being ground-ward. I inched my way to the commode. When I got there, I finger-crawled the wall and pulled myself up by rails bolted between the toilet and shower. Is this what prying your way out of an avalanche is like? Pinned and with nothing but weary breath to live by.

With that same perseverance, I failed to nurse my son.

The nurse arrived. She laid Keats in his terrarium-like cradle, helped me out of bed, and to the bathroom. I splashed my face with cold water. I dragged a soapy wash-cloth over my body. I tried to avoid looking at my reflection in the mirror; I caught a glimpse of the pallid stranger wearing the ratty gray robe. My hair fell over my shoulders, snarled and in need of washing. Mom. Why hadn't I asked Mom to shampoo my hair, to brush it before she left? We'd have shared an intimacy, one I knew she craved. I pictured my mother sitting behind me, pulling through knots.

The nurse helped me back to bed. "The baby can't eat," I said. "And his arm. He barely moves."

"Bring him over." The nurse eased Keats back to me. "Look." I repeated our latch-dance. Nothing changed.

"He'll want you more if he's cold." She smiled at Keats, as a person smiles at a child who has done a foolish thing. "Undress him. A clothed baby is a lazy baby. And his arm is fine."

"I remember," I said, "from the girls." I turned the word *lazy* over as I stripped my son. *Lazy* is a common description for a baby slow to nurse. Keats wasn't lazy. He didn't know how to be. Lazy means not trying. I can't think of a more valiant and rigorous feat than withstand-ing that great squeeze, from the comforting, unknowing blackness of a mother's body and into cold, endless-bright, unforgiving air. I ran my finger over Keats's throat and down to his navel. I wondered if he felt bruised all over like I did. I wondered if he was lazy with pain, like me.

Keats wanted it. He was red with hunger. He flexed his hands and rubbed his eyes and tried again to latch. He tried so hard.

The nurse shrugged. I needed to practice. "Keep trying," she said. "Give it time." She patted my leg like you pat a good dog. She left Keats empty-bellied and yowling.

There was a sinking in me. Did Keats know? Was it written on my body? My milk bitter with past?

EVENING WORE INTO night. Once day-green trees were traced silver with moon. The brush and grasses beyond the window swayed with wind, noiseless as a field mouse. Tony had come and gone. He promised he'd be back for us soon, after he put Jo to bed.

I was learning Keats, going over every sumptuous inch of baby. The tips of his ears pointed. His second toe was longest. His hair grew up from his neck and down from the crown of his head. His fingers peeled between, skin like pith. His torso long. His belly plump. His mouth a bow like mine is bowed. I closed my eyes. I pictured Keats smiling. Gummy and wide and tooth-ridged. In my son's future smile, the miracle of the return; of me, his strong mother. There's a moment not too far from now. I'm whole again and grinning back at Keats. Our mirror smiles. A thousand years from now, someone will have Keats's smile too. Nobody will know where it came from.

Back to his body. To the ridge of his spine, bumped beneath my finger like rope. And his chin and neck, creamy folds of baby flesh, yellowed from yesterday, the color of goldenrod. And his right arm, it flapped down at his side, immobile, like a broken wing. I pushed the call button again. Maybe I was imagining his body trouble, like a magnifying glass sees the small and inconsequential. I wasn't taking any risks. I'd rather be mouthy and needy of the nurse than sorry. A pediatrician had looked him over. She certified his health and discharge. "What a healthy boy he is," I was told.

Keats had been handed to doctors and nurses both, been taken for hearing tests, and diapered, and patted over. Surely, someone would've taken notice of a problem with his arm. I asked the late-shift nurse anyway. "And his skin," I said. "He's jaundiced?" She unwrapped Keats and unzipped his too-large newborn-size jammies.

"Yes," she said. "Yes." She ordered a test to measure Keats's bilirubin level, the yellow serum in blood that forms as cells break down and filter through the liver. Newborns often have elevated bilirubin levels. Their livers aren't mature, or they're dehydrated waiting for their mother's milk to come in. Yellowing skin and eyes are a hallmark of jaundice. "No need to panic," the nurse told me. She took Keats away for the test. Not long after, she returned.

Keats had very high levels of bilirubin in his blood, a fraction of a percent below needing phototherapy—a treatment with ultraviolet light.

Early the next morning, Keats's bilirubin levels were even higher.

But a doctor ordered us home. There was no room in the overcrowded hospital to keep us.

I was still unable to walk, still unable to pick Keats up on my own. Keats was now tawny and slow to respond to touch. And as he slept, he stopped breathing for moments, then gasped himself awake, startled from lack of air. And still no latch. I was given a case of formula to help him along. I was glad to have it, to nourish him in any way I could.

Our midwife came to say goodbye, wearing a look of defeat and humiliation. The hospital could move us to a different floor, a unit treating ill people, exposing Keats to their germs. "But Keats is compromised," I said. "He's not eating. He's jaundiced." The midwife was apologetic. She knew it was wrong to make us leave, Keats so lethargic and yellow. I wondered if it would cost her her job to speak up. The midwife wrote me a script for a walker. A gesture both touching and taunting. I needed help. Keats needed the lights.

I demanded to speak with a supervisor. The charge nurse entered the room, her face stiffened. I told her I wasn't going anywhere. She told me I'd be going upstairs to the sick floor if we stayed. Two grown women arguing, trading back-and-forth barbs over a helpless baby. Keats could barely move, and not for his size and age, but from some condition, I thought. But it didn't matter what I said. We were going. Maybe it was best to pry my son from the grips of this medicine.

We packed to leave. My hair in knots. Dried blood streaked my legs. I could barely hobble to the bathroom. I yelled at every nurse, staff member, and doctor I saw. "I'm a writer," I warned them. "Do something."

Writers tell.

But the threat of words was nothing next to the reality of not enough resources.

My boy, my bird, my Keats; midnight eyes at the brim, he looked like a hatchling forced ruthlessly from the nest.

20

We drove Keats home. The girls ran to the front door as our car rolled into the driveway. Four small hands smudging glass. Tony unbuckled Keats from his car seat and carried him in. Jo and Iris rushed Daddy and Keats, like they were celebrities. Mom took my suitcase, turned to carry it upstairs.

Tony passed Keats over to me. I laid him on the floor on a navy blue receiving blanket printed with white whales spouting water. Keats wriggled his legs and curled his toes and punched the air with his left arm. His right arm was still limp, as if strapped to his side. *Nothing's wrong*, I told myself. Keats was figuring out how to live in his body, how to make it go.

Down on the floor, he cried, asking to be held. Jo

wanted him. Jo would charm him. She sat in a cream-colored armchair, right in the middle, ready. I looked at Tony and Mom to ascertain whether Jo was ready. "Baby," she cooed. "Here I am." Keats seemed to hurt less when held; his body needed bracing. "He's ouchy." Jo was matter-of-fact. "Give him."

Jo cradled Keats. She pushed his shoulder gently in, whispering her secrets. He quieted. He reached a hand toward her face, feeling for her. He couldn't see far, but he could smell Jo, feel her. Sister. There was no doubt after, then and now. Keats belongs to Jo. Her name was his first word. He runs around the house, "Jo! Jo! Jo!" his voice scratchy and guttural.

And after the greetings and bonding were well started and all family to bed that first at-home night, I pulled Keats to me. He struggled with my nipple, rolling it around with his tongue and then out of his mouth. I pushed my nipple between his lips and squeezed. Milk was in. My breasts were hot and round, the size of grapefruits, and streaked with purple stretch marks. Baby to breast is symbiotic, a moving from body to body. A feed relieves pressure and pain. White dribbled down Keats's chin and onto my thighs, none of it into his belly. He gagged from the force of my milk and from hunger.

I felt my way through the unlit room, rummaging through a drawer I'd stocked with bottles. It's advised to wait to give a newborn a bottle. They might suffer nipple confusion and never take the breast. But I had to try.

I hooked myself to my breast pump, expressed the milk stretching me full. A cone over each breast, pulling and pulling. Keats's latch had rubbed me raw. Blood-spattered milk pattered into collection vials. Each filled quickly, the color of strawberry Quik.

I poured the milk into the bottle and screwed the cap tight. Keats cried from his co-sleeper between Tony and me. I turned to Tony, pink milk in hand. The room was violet, daybreak through blinds like a wound. Everything hurt. My labor-worn body. The crook of my arm where the IV needle had lived, now a low-grade ache on sunset-hued skin. Keats squirmed beneath a straightjacket-tight swaddle. His bed was a taupe-colored puffed ring. It looked like a raft, something to pull behind a boat. I pushed Tony's shoulder. He didn't budge. "Hey," I grouched. "Wake up." Me up all night, how could Tony sleep?

"What? What?" Tony muttered, groggy, half-awake.

I stared at him, eyes glazed over with panic. I pulled Keats from his little raft and unbound him from his blanket. His flesh was hot to the touch and looked honey-dipped. "Sorry to wake you." I was gentle with Tony now. "It's just, he can't eat." I pulled my nightgown down at the neck, showing Tony my breast. It was hard and swollen, milk-letting as Keats cried. My body needed him, as his needed mine.

"He's fine," Tony said. "You always think there's something wrong. Go back to sleep." He turned over, his back to me, toes poking out of blankets like parched stems in a bouquet. Keats had been up three times to feed and had gotten no milk.

"Just because you want him to be fine, that doesn't make it true." But Tony was already asleep. I'd breastfed two babies for too many years to count. This was different. Keats panicked at my breast.

His first real take was blood-mixed milk. I brought the bottle to Keats's mouth. The nipple wouldn't part his lips. He clamped on that too, taking near nothing. I turned the nipple in, like a screw, rotating it beyond his gums and over his tongue. He took long, hungry gulps, went too fast. The milk came up from him, pink all over us both. And now he was really crying, deep despair from such a small body. I laid him down in the raft again and walked through the dark room and into our bathroom. I flipped the switch. The wiring was faulty. The bulbs flicked on and off, on and off, like a child playing with the lights.

I rummaged the medicine cabinet and found a syringe. I brought it over to my babe. I filled the plastic with my remaining milk. I held Keats against me and fed him one drop at a time. The milk quieted him. I was crying now.

21

A few nights later, Tony flew away to California on a red-eye. He'd not be home until July. I'd summoned all of my women to help. My mother, my aunt, and my best friend from college would rotate days. It was all hands on deck. I was embarrassed to have had to ask, not for their company, but for the admission asking made. There was no pretty face to paint on this.

Keats and I shared the bed the night Tony left. Summer's heat wave was ongoing. The air conditioner still broken, our house stayed a steady eighty-five degrees. A ceiling fan whirred above us, pushing hot air from one side of the room to the other. I worried for my right sense in that temperature, I was so jagged from lack of sleep. Anything seemed possible. It was as if the heat and the

humidity were conspiring against me. The room was spot-
less, sanitized. It smelled like baking-soda carpet cleaner
and Pine-Sol. Mom had been cleaning all week, couldn't
stop tidying. She said if she let herself sit, she worried she
wouldn't be able to quit yelling at Tony. I imagined my
tiny mother laying into him. And I liked it.

The alarm clock rang at midnight. I hurried to quiet
the chime. Keats had just fussed himself to sleep. A fight
to the finish. I don't know how he managed on such an
empty stomach. I'd tried to force the bottle again, pressing two fingers against his tongue to jam it in. But Keats
had immediately clamped down, choking as the bottle
squirted milk around his mouth and down his throat. I
was afraid to move. Afraid to wake him. I didn't have it in
me to rock him back to sleep. I was pumping milk every
two hours during the day, and waking at night to pump
too. I worried my milk would dry if I missed a squeezing. I
had no other purpose. I was not a person. I was an energy
in a shell peering through eyeholes. I inched my way out
of bed toward the pump, so all was still, the baby at peace.
But what is that feeling? I thought. I'd been clenching. My
teeth clamped so tight they ached. Now there was a pain
in my jaw like chewing broken glass. I cupped my hands
in front of me. I spit. Little bits of white rolled around my
palm. My molar, crumbled to the root.

I took Keats to the pediatrician in the morning. His
blood needed to be drawn to check bilirubin levels. The

results of tests the days before showed he was a hair away from needing to be hospitalized, not really getting better. I begged the doctor to give my boy light therapy that morning. "What kind of mother wants their child in the hospital?" she chastised. The doctor told me to place Keats in the sun beneath a window at home.

It was too hot to put Keats in the sun. Later, I lay naked in bed with Keats across my chest, him in nothing but a diaper, our sweat running together. Unclothed, I walked him over to the window and put us both in the light, moving in and out so the heat couldn't touch him. I didn't think about the neighbors. I held my baby son and it felt like I was a skydiver pulling the ripcord. We were falling together and I couldn't hold him hard enough. He was going down on my watch, just like Cara did. I was in a haunted place, in my home and in my body. I bargained. I couldn't let that darkness touch my son. My love, she died; but we were still here.

Keats's little head tipped back and over my arm. The fact of him almost made me believe in something bigger than that moment, the beyond. If I believed, there was a reason for all of this pain. And at the bottom of my life, that fantasy held me like I held Keats. I prayed to the past and hoped it would spare him.

I love my son. I love how his hair is a kind of fuzz, a downy, sparse, and unnamable shade of brown. I love his sable eyes and long toes and blond lashes. I love the bald spot on his head from where it met his mattress. I hold him sometimes and it feels like we're breathing together. We're body travelers sharing the answer to the world's greatest riddle, and the riddle's answer is love.

For Keats, truth, and beauty.

22

Thirteen days of newborn life. The doctors didn't know what was wrong. I placed Keats on a pediatric scale to be weighed. A nurse measured his head, then stuck his heel with a tiny needle. She squeezed blood from his foot into a vial. Keats cried and shook. He'd known so much discomfort in so few days. The doctor looked him over. She said he was perfectly healthy. Nothing out of place. Nothing broken. Nothing strained. My milk was the problem. If I gave Keats formula, he'd be fine. "No," I said. "Let me show you." I pulled a bottle of formula from a diaper bag. I took Keats into my arms and tilted him back, trying to fit his mouth with the nipple. He turned his head from side to side, refusing to drink, as he did at home. "I'll come back later." The doctor opened the door to leave. "He's just shy."

I called our midwife and explained Keats's symptoms. The weight loss. The yellow skin. My baby immobile and exhausted. She saw us the same day. I was so relieved to see her, I pushed Keats into her arms. She brought me to the closet-size room where she slept for minutes at a time between checking laboring patients. The bed was topped with a brown fuzzy blanket. Cans of soda lined her mini fridge. She offered me one. We sat on separate ends of the bed.

She forced Keats's mouth open with her thumb, rolling her index finger over his tongue and beneath his top and bottom lips. She nodded knowingly. "He's double-tied." She shook her head. "Pediatricians discount problems with latch." She was visibly angry. "It's hard to hold them first and then leave them. I can't help him out there."

Keats couldn't latch at all, no matter what we tried. Without surgery, he'd struggle to eat and his speech would likely be impaired. The midwife referred us to a dental surgery center in Pittsburgh. She saved my son.

Ten months later, two months before her retirement, she was fired from the hospital where I birthed Keats. I've heard it argued that midwives are an insurance risk, yet births attended by midwives have statistically lower rates of cesarean section; labors that cost less make fewer dollars. And anyway, in West Virginia, employers don't need to give a reason for letting a worker go. Without her pension, after years of service, she packed to leave.

———

ANNA, ONE OF my graduate students, drove with Keats and me to the surgery center in Pittsburgh. We chatted the whole way. The front of my shirt was milk-sour. Anna pretended not to notice. She's from Alabama. She could curse your mother out and it would sound polite, insult smothered in syrup. Keats slept in the back seat. He was so tiny, his pants covered his feet. We made the two-hour drive. Anna told me who was sleeping with whom, and that her husband smokes cigars and had a gun in the house (she liked that). We talked about her memoir, and how afraid she was to hurt her mother and brother. I assured her that writing is a service, not an act of aggression but of love. People need to be seen and heard. I implored her to remember, to follow the path of bravery, not fear.

As a professor, I'd always considered myself the fourth wall. That day I stepped out from behind it and into a surgery center. Anna held Keats as I filled out his intake forms.

A nurse called me and Anna in, thinking we were a couple. We went along with it. That was easier than explaining. There were two doctors, both with bright white teeth. One doctor strapped Keats into a papoose on a surgical table. He laid hands on Keats as if he were putting together a valuable broken thing. He pulled a surgical lamp over. The diagnosis: a severe lip and tongue–tie. The midwife was right. "There will be a moment of pain," he said. "Keats won't remember a thing. You, you're a different story."

I was asked to leave the room for the procedure. It was over in fifteen minutes. The nurse carried Keats back to me. He was bundled in blue, new as morning. I took him into my arms. His little face was so warm against my chest. The nurse told me how beautifully he'd done. Keats didn't cry or try to break free. He turned toward the light.

23

Independence Day. Keats was three weeks old. Tony flew home to help us pack for our upcoming months in California. Many things we needed were still stowed in boxes. There'd been so little time to unpack at the new rental.

Josephine helped make a bowl cake that morning: fresh strawberries, blueberries from the bush, and vanilla batter from scratch. At dusk, Tony dragged a match against the striker and ignited black snakes and Pharaoh's serpents, button-size disks that uncoil in ash and crawl with smoke and heat. Sparklers lit the holiday. Jo gripped one in each hand. She wrote her name in loops against the sky. The town shot fireworks off by the river. There were two, then three, then four. Color all over.

Iris was just stringing sentences together, always

copying the adults. She didn't want a sparkler. She hid behind me, buried her face in my legs. "Oh dear," she said. "No good." Roman candles shot over the river and fell down like sinking stones.

When I was a little girl, Fourth of July was the start of the new year. Fire washed the sky clean. "See," I said to Tony. "It's not so bad here. There are beautiful things." It was the beautiful things that crushed me most; they came seemingly out of nowhere and beckoned me to stay.

Keats lay in his crib upstairs, well-fed now but yellow and listless, the Fourth of July exploding the sky around. Fire blooms covered the moon. Tony and Iris and Jo and I waited for the grand finale. The force of the blasts obscured Jo's cheering; the glory of golds and reds and blues gone. I read her lips. "Mommy!" Jo pointed to the sky. "This is America. Isn't it perfect?"

A WEEK LATER, we left West Virginia for California and Tony's job. I hoped our departure would offer the time I needed to understand all that had happened with our baby and my body.

Keats's four-week checkup. Late by a week.

In Los Angeles, the doctor ran her finger over Keats's clavicle. She stopped when she felt a hard lump between Keats's chest and shoulder. "Of course, you know his clavicle is broken." I shook my head no. "A hard birth?"

But yes, I thought. *Yes.*

I brushed my fingertips over the contours of the knot. A bone callus had grown and drawn the fracture together. It was smooth and pitted, like a drusy pearl. His shoulder must've hooked my pelvic bone during his birth.

The doctor held my hand in place, over the scar.

"Here."

PART FIVE

And yet—when one begins to search
for the crucial, the definitive moment,
the moment which changed all others,
one finds oneself pressing, in great pain,
through a maze of false signals and
abruptly locking doors.

James Baldwin, *Giovanni's Room*

24

I did a shameful thing. My first autumn in West Virginia, I mentored Kat. She had candy-red hair, a smile both sly and trampled, and hailed from Ohio. Not long into our first semester, Kat published an essay in an online journal featuring stories about MFA programs. Kat wrote about the pleasures and pains of Morgantown. Our community of writers. The natural world. Her walk to campus past human shit on the Walnut Street Bridge, opioid users dying beneath. Kat wrote about her neighbor. He beat his wife; night after night of dull thumping through their shared wall. She'd called the police and watched from her window as the patrol wrestled her neighbor onto their duplex's green lawn. Jailed for one night, the neighbor was home the day after next, right on the other side of the wall

again. Kat slept with a knife under her pillow after. That's
what her essay said.

The last time I saw Kat was at Keats's baby shower. I
was eight months along—you know the story of me then.
My graduate students had insisted on putting the party
on. I needed to be reminded to celebrate, they'd said, and
asked if we could use my house. Nobody in their cohort
had room to host. I hadn't told them what had happened
with the pregnancy, how hard it had been. Boxes and
boxes of baby gifts filled my living room. Onesies printed
with bears. Bibs stitched with red anchors and blue ships.
Plush lions that rattled. Kat brought an elegant blue glass
pitcher with a gold handle, university colors, crafted of
Blenko glass. That West Virginia company was founded
right outside of Morgantown, in Point Marion, Pennsylvania, now famous for blown-glass houseware, modern art.
"For you," she said. "A little color. In case you forget you
deserve nice things." Kat put her arm around my shoulder. "But I think you know."

I turned the pitcher over, ran my finger along its
crowned edge. Astonished is too small a word. I couldn't
even speak.

I taught nonfiction writing. It was my job to help students make sense of the truth. And what did I say to Kat
our first year in Morgantown, so many lifetimes ago? I told
Kat when I was in grad school in Newark, people were
stabbed in the library. *Stabbed*, and I never complained. In
other words: shut it, or good students won't come here.

West Virginia is a negative growth state. More people die or leave than are born and stay. Kat's written words felt like a threat to community good, though I knew they were true. If people saw her (real) version of Morgantown, I feared they'd fail to see beyond the bleak take. There was the feeling among my town friends that we were in it together, bound as comrades in combat. It was an intoxicating allegiance, one hard to abandon and painful to betray.

My life was divided, before and after Morgantown. Mention of the fine qualities of other places wasn't done. Neither was airing our dirty laundry. It didn't matter what worked and was good outside. We should greet the concept of tomorrow with optimism. Tomorrow will be better. Tomorrow can change yesterday. This is what we had, what *was*. The price of community. I paid it. I asked Kat to pay it too. And it hurt for me to do that. She was ashamed for the right thing she wrote, because of my disapproval. And I let her be.

How fast I'd fallen into place.

Silence came naturally to me. My mother taught me loyalty. Always protect the vulnerable and those you love, no matter the cost. Sometimes shielding a person requires silence; we hide the ugly bits so the beautiful ones can surface. I loved West Virginia as if she were mine and long-lost.

For years and years outsiders have taken what they wanted from the state. They've turned profits through photographs of ruin and tales of woe. Appalachian land is poisoned by industry for the whole country's benefit: chemicals, coal, lumber, and railroads. Companies come. They move on when there's nothing left to take. Imagine every ancient tree on every mountaintop felled. All the native spruce gone. People die for electricity, to provide power for the rest of us. Those coal stacks in Morgantown, for example: they power New Jersey. West Virginians eat and drink that smoke. This story is a reverse of the mentioned history, though. I'm an outsider, but I didn't take from West Virginia nearly as much as I left myself there.

What does it take to be of a place? I was born in Upstate New York. I can tell you all about the Empire State's darkness. I belong to it and it belongs to me. Maybe citizenship requires a native tongue. We're kindred with our first word: dog, or mama, or milk. I gave my body to West Virginia. I let blood on a Morgantown labor room floor, my hope and worry and ache came out. I gave West Virginia a son; his first breath, his first cry, roaring from my body to life. Babies are born into togetherness. Months pass until they understand they are separate, a person apart from their mothers. We left West Virginia for California. I wondered when we got there how I'd ever explain to Keats. He belongs to West Virginia and I do not. Outsider. One of the great pains of my life, separate from my son that way.

West, by God, Virginia. That's what she's called. West Virginia's official state motto is *Montani Semper Liberi* (Latin for "Mountaineers Are Always Free"). After moving to West Virginia, I learned many people outside don't even know it's a state. They think it's Virginia's western arm. A place off Interstate 95 on the way to the beach. "West, by God, Virginia!" is the unofficial state motto. It serves as a correction. Mountaineers yell it in bars and on the streets and in churches, countering the assumption they are invisibles, people from nowhere in a nothing place.

I tuned in to my old neighbor Kirk on West Virginia public radio not long ago, all the way from California. I'm always listening in, still longing. You leave a place that hurts you, part of you remains; lover and prisoner.

Kirk parsed "West, by God" on the program, contemplating its origin, a thing often puzzled over and that nobody seems to know the answer to. Kirk said the *Virginia Spectator* first published the phrase in a story written by students at the University of Virginia during Prohibition, in reference to moonshine and how to cut it to get a woman drunk. To have their way. Kirk's voice has a subtle and gentle drawl. My neighbor, no longer my neighbor, a thing that produces in me a deep ache. He read from the *Spectator*, "And it is, we believe, the only way that corn can be mixed and presented to a girl—except the iron plated ones from West (by God) Virginia." The women of West Virginia held spirit best. They're resilient, always will be.

My mother grew up in a nine-hundred-square-foot, two-bedroom house in Albany, New York. The last of five children, Mom was the unintended voyager of parents in their forties. Her father was a house painter. Her mother was a house cook. Nobody went to college. Her grandparents were Sicilian fruit farmers, nothing ever squandered or risked.

I never met my grandmother. She died the year before I was born. But I've always pictured her standing in her too-small Orlando Avenue kitchen, staring through the tiny square window that faced the scrubby-grassed backyard, round with my mother, wondering how they'd afford a fifth, only seventeen months between babies. My grandmother was a good Catholic, on her feet all day in kitchens during the week and at church on the weekends. The women in my family worked hard, and I've never forgotten how their sacrifice allowed me the life I've led. The education. The travel. The children. The privilege to teach for a living, to use my mind.

For my mother and my grandmother, I promised myself when I was young, after my abortion, that as soon as I could I'd leave home.

I promised myself I'd never go back. But we always go back.

I grew up knowing nothing about the Sicily we came from. Ours was an Ellis Island arrival. The picture goes black after. People who'd remember in my family are dead. My mother lost both parents before she was twenty-one. Her brothers are dead. They were the eldest siblings, the only ones who talked to the many aunts and uncles from Italy now passed. Our family rushed to assimilate. There had been poverty and hardship in Italy; all that was past held that stain. Emigrating offered a chance at a better life. We never talked about it before, so that we might be Americans someday.

From a distance now, I see. Pieces of my history patterned, laid one by one like a jigsaw, revealing the predrawn picture. We leave like birds, home-going by earth-slant and heat change. We journey by light: star, sun, moon. Over oceans and mountains and cities. Not by memory, by nature. We don't choose the destination, we feel it.

We'd moved from California to West Virginia, a place I'd never been, and never dreamed I'd go, far yet familiar. There was a scratching in me, soft, like a rodent in the wall, easy to ignore, asking to be heard and let into the warm house. And I answered.

I learned state history. Sicilians worked West Virginia's glory days. The state was built on the backs of immigrants; Italians arrived between 1820 and the early 1900s. Coal bosses promised better, lured them with lies. Perilous conditions in Italy's sulfur mines were replaced with perilous conditions in West Virginia's coal mines.

West Virginia refers to itself in counties; some towns house only a family or two. Italians settled the state. Marion County, Harrison County, Tucker County, Randolph County, Preston County, McDowell County, and Monongalia County—where Morgantown is. Most Italians not in coal worked the trades as carpenters, shoemakers, stone masons, glassblowers, and blacksmiths. The Great Depression rolled in. Jobs were scarce. Italians fled West Virginia for northern states: Connecticut, New Jersey, and New York.

The summer we moved to West Virginia, I unpacked the last of our boxes, and not long after drove through misty mountains to New York. To Mom.

Mom had a box waiting for me. She walked upstairs and into the attic, a little door that opens into a sun-hot eave. She carried down a large plastic container holding her dead brother's belongings. He'd been into genealogy at the end. Mom pushed the container over to my side of the table, the only worldly things Mom had of her brother's inside.

We rooted through it together. Mom said her grandfather had wanted to be a painter. Instead, he worked as a glassblower. All day he stooped over, torching color into vases for rich people. In the box, a map folded into a square. I opened it, spread it over the table. It was a crude illustration of the town where her grandfather had first lived and worked and stayed for twenty years, the place he'd come to from Sicily. The town was circled in thick orange, a compass and ruler drawn beside. He'd moved to the border, the land between Point Marion and Morgantown, ten miles from my new front door. West Virginia. I was home.

Our Hopecrest house sat atop a hill. Deer slept on our front lawn, like in a fairy tale. Cardinals sang so loudly at sunup I had to close the windows in order to sleep. Red birds perched on a power wire strung between trees. They stared blankly at me as I drew the blinds. Fireflies numbered in the thousands the summer Keats was born; Jo and Iris chased after them, barefoot, Mason jars in hand. Wildflowers blossomed everywhere. Honeysuckle perfume was sweeter than cake.

Autumn's foliage falls and the view from Hopecrest changes. Where there'd been leaf cover, the town's waste transfer station flanks the river, spewing acrid fumes that smell like burning tires. As if the station hadn't been there all summertime and forever. Coal and gravel trucks plow through town day and night. The deer pretty on the lawn are dead along the highway.

In *Ways of Seeing*, John Berger writes, "The relation between what we see and what we know is never settled. Each evening we see the sun set. We know that the earth is turning away from it. Yet the knowledge, the explanation, never quite fits the sight." In this way, my motherhood and West Virginia orbit the same star, planets opposed, casting the other in shadow.

Writing this book, some might say I've perpetrated an unforgivable taboo. I've voiced the unspeakable. For state and for child. But I had to. Because we got to California and Keats never could nurse; surgery was too late to repair his latch (I milked myself by machine for eight hours a day, for four months, and then my milk dried), and because Keats suffered the agony of a broken bone and I didn't know, and because I didn't know I couldn't help him. And that is how my son entered this world, with a mother who couldn't answer his pain. And that led me to think of all the other babies out there, how we've failed them. And that is where I went each sleepless California night, a new-born boy waking every other hour to feed. I'd turn the bottle past his lips like a screw. In and In and In.

Josephine, Iris, and Keats don't belong to me. I belong to them. I am here to nurture and protect, to teach them how to be in the world. Love is a word not strong enough to describe what I feel. But it's a word anti-choice laws and activists use to trap mothers. They bind us with shame and they weaponize our love. They count on us to stay quiet. If I admit to not having wanted to be pregnant with Keats, I wound my son. I deny him of his rightful mother-love. It's a propaganda running so deep, it's difficult to see it for what it is. Choice is complex. I can both want to have had rea-sonable access to abortion *and* love and want my son.

Choice bolsters the miraculous attachment we have to our babies. If we bring our children into life with our agency intact, we remain strong enough to raise them in this world of wolves. Mothers lead by example. If I say nothing of choice, what do I teach my son about what his sisters need and deserve? What will I tell my daugh-ters about what I did to protect their health? What will my children want when they're older—a mother who played nice, or a mother who fought?

I think you know.

ACKNOWLEDGMENTS

This book was made possible with generous support from The MacDowell Colony, The Brown Foundation Fellows Program at the Dora Maar House, the Corporation of Yaddo, and West Virginia University's Eberly College of the Arts. And Nancy Sernas.

ABOUT THE AUTHOR

CHRISTA PARRAVANI is the bestselling author of *Her: A Memoir*. She has taught at Dartmouth College, UMass Amherst, SUNY Purchase, and West Virginia University, where she served as an assistant professor of creative nonfiction. She earned her MFA in visual art from Columbia University and her MFA in creative writing from Rutgers University–Newark.